A Practic... Road ...

A Practical Approach to Road Traffic Law

Susan Cavender, *Barrister, Guildhall Chambers*

Alistair Haggerty, *Barrister, Guildhall Chambers*

Bloomsbury Professional

LONDON · DUBLIN · EDINBURGH · NEW YORK · NEW DELHI · SYDNEY

BLOOMSBURY PROFESSIONAL

Bloomsbury Publishing Plc
50 Bedford Square, London, WC1B 3DP, UK
1385 Broadway, New York, NY 10018, USA
29 Earlsfort Terrace, Dublin 2, Ireland

BLOOMSBURY and the Diana logo are trademarks of Bloomsbury Publishing Plc

British Library Cataloguing-in-Publication Data

A catalogue record for this book is available from the British Library.

	ISBN:	PB:	978 1 52652 185 9
		Epdf:	978 1 52652 187 3
		Epub:	978 1 52652 186 6

Typeset by Evolution Design and Digital (Kent)
Printed and bound by CPI Group (UK) Ltd, Croydon, CR0 4YY

To find out more about our authors and books visit www.bloomsburyprofessional.com. Here you will find extracts, author information, details of forthcoming events and the option to sign up for our newsletters

Foreword

Road traffic law affects us all, whether we are motorists, cyclists, public transport users, pedestrians or – like many of us – each of the above. In a densely populated country we all encounter the roads somehow, regulation is essential, and there is a high risk of being on one side or the other of a contravention.

Road traffic law is also something of which many lawyers have at least some professional experience. For a few, it is a specialist area. For others, it is part of a portfolio. For a lot of us, it is an area in which we learned the art and craft of advocacy, at first instance and on appeal.

My first reported case can be found in the Road Traffic Reports for 1985. It was an appeal to the Divisional Court in a case about parking. I learned a little about parking law and rather more about appellate advocacy. But that case was the exception. More common was to defend or mitigate before the magistrates in a case of speeding or some other moving traffic offence. I have memories, less than fond, of traipsing off to some distant court in the hope of persuading the Bench not to disqualify my client, all for a fee that barely covered the cost of my journey there and back.

I wish I had been in possession of this book at the time. It would have allowed me swiftly to discover that a defendant who wants to argue special reasons or exceptional hardship needs to call evidence (Chapter 21). That would have avoided one embarrassing stumble. The book would also have guided me on the imposition of penalty points, where this is discretionary. That, in the 1980s, was an even more complex process than it is now, and somewhat random. Road traffic lawyers should be very grateful to the Sentencing Council, which has established clear guidelines, and to the authors of this book, who give clear and concise advice on the right approach to points and endorsement (Chapter 21).

As a barrister I was lucky enough to avoid a case in which my client was at risk of both immediate custody and a driving disqualification. But I was vaguely aware that this was a problem area. The main difficulty was that in some such cases the offender could benefit from serving all or part of his disqualification whilst in custody. This issue was not tackled until 2009, when Parliament added ss 35A and 35B to the Road Traffic Offenders Act 1988. It was another six years before those sections were brought into force. Their aim is straightforward: to ensure that the appropriate disqualification period is served outside custody. The method sounds simple: to extend the disqualification by the period of time the offender will spend in custody. But in practice this can be tricky.

I know this because in recent years I have come back to road traffic law, sitting in the Court of Appeal (Criminal Division). A remarkable number of sentencing appeals from the Crown Court feature some kind of issue arising from s 35A or 35B. Although in *Needham* (2016) the court explained those provisions in detail, difficulties persist. This book addresses the issue with clarity (see Chapter 14). It is to be hoped that this will reduce the number of glitches we see.

The book also contains a great deal of helpful advice for advocates. The Survival Guide that opens the book will be invaluable to the novice. Chapter 6 contains much useful practical guidance. Elsewhere, the authors have shared top tips on specific aspects of the job, such as handling expert witnesses at trial and opening the facts for sentence. I would strongly endorse the point made in Chapter 18 – that a prosecutor opening the facts for sentence should not simply read from the police summary, which is prepared at an early stage of the case for a different purpose. In the Crown Court, at least, the advocate who does this may find that the judge has a better grasp of the relevant facts than the prosecutor.

All these points reflect features of an earlier book from the same stable: *Practical Advocacy in the Crown Court*. I commend this latest venture in what looks like becoming a series.

By the way, although books like this are not made for browsing, the idle reader might find something of interest, as I did when preparing this foreword. I was unaware of the CPS list of examples of what might amount to careless driving (paragraph **11.14**). I shall find it of some comfort next time I am upset by being overtaken on the inside.

Mark Warby LJ
Royal Courts of Justice
Strand
London WC2A 2LL

Preface

Most of us have experience of being a driver or passenger in a car on an almost daily basis, so it is hardly surprising that road traffic cases are some of the most frequently encountered in everyday criminal practice. For many people, the only time that they have any experience of the criminal justice system is when they fall foul of the law governing their use of the roads.

Approximately 32 million people hold a full car driving licence in England, and many others hold HGV or taxi licences as well. The implications of breaching the rules and regulations, whether on a major or minor scale, are in play whenever we get behind the wheel of a vehicle.

Road traffic law is wide-ranging, sometimes complex, and occasionally required in tragic circumstances. Lawyers at every level are involved; prosecuting or defending people who have been caught up in the criminal justice system in the many and varied cases, ranging from those who trigger a speed camera to those who cause death by dangerous driving.

Whilst there already exist a number of hefty and erudite books about road traffic law (*Wilkinson's on Road Traffic Offences* remains the indispensable text book on the subject), the aim of this book is to provide a user-friendly and practical guide. We have drawn together, in a simple and easy-to-use format, those aspects of road traffic law which most commonly arise in day-to-day court practice, whilst also providing information about slightly more rarefied areas such as heavy goods vehicles and taxis which crop up in the magistrates' courts surprisingly often.

In addition to providing solicitors and barristers with a handy courtroom guide, this book will assist the increasing number of people who choose to represent themselves in court. By setting out the law, procedure and guidelines in a practical and easy-to-access manner, it is hoped that this book will be a useful aid to legal practitioners and members of the public alike.

The chapters in this book will assist you with preparing and presenting a case at every stage. In addition to setting out the relevant law and procedure, the authors provide advice on delivering persuasive and effective advocacy, tailored to the nature of the case and the tribunal deciding the outcome.

This is a practical guide, and its emphasis is on practical application. You will not find a detailed academic analysis of the law, or lengthy anecdotes from practitioners, in this book. Our hope is that it will instead ensure that you have the tools that you need in court. It should serve as an essential guide to the law and successfully presenting your case.

Preface

The book has been written by a combination of authors, drawn from both the solicitor and barrister arms of the legal profession, all of whom have considerable familiarity with road traffic law. The chapters are the product of their collective knowledge, experience and wisdom and will, we hope, ensure that you are well prepared when you step into court.

On behalf of all the authors of this book, we would like to thank our families and colleagues for their support in putting it together. Some of them have assisted with proof reading, and many more provided equally welcome cups of tea and words of encouragement. We are especially grateful to Caighli Taylor for her invaluable advice and ideas, without which this book would not have been possible.

Susan Cavender
Alistair Haggerty
September 2022

Contents

Contents

Contributors

Susan Cavender: Susan has been a barrister with Guildhall Chambers since 2004, having started professional life as a solicitor in Soho. She covers a wide range of criminal prosecution and defence cases including road traffic offences, regulatory work and is a liquor licensing specialist.

Alistair Haggerty: Alistair (2012 call) prosecutes and defends in a wide range of criminal cases and has an established practice in health and safety and environmental law. He has been instructed by companies and individuals, including some high-profile clients, in the full spectrum of driving cases.

Nicholas Lee: Nicholas is a specialist criminal barrister at Guildhall Chambers, Bristol. He prosecutes and defends in cases across the criminal spectrum, including road traffic offences

Darren Burleigh: Darren specialises in defending regulatory and criminal cases including motoring matters, with particular experience in the road haulage sector. He Joined the Roll of Solicitors at the beginning of 1995 and is now a Director at Star Legal.

Grace Flynn: Called to the bar in 2015, Grace practised in criminal defence and prosecution at Guildhall Chambers before joining Capsticks LLP where she now specialises in cases of professional misconduct. She has also worked in house at West Midlands and Staffordshire Police. Her grandfather owned an MOT garage and would have been delighted to see her write a chapter on this topic one day. She still owns the Fiat Panda that she passed her driving test in.

Mandla Ndlovu: Mandla was called to the bar in 2015 and is a criminal barrister with Guildhall Chambers. He covers the full gamut of criminal offences, both defending and prosecuting. Mandla has experience driving vehicles on land and water as he currently lives on a canal boat.

Jack Barry: Jack is a criminal and regulatory barrister with Queen Square Chambers. Called to the Bar in 2021 he completed pupillage with a nationally-recognised firm of solicitors before joining Chambers in July 2022. He is a keen writer with articles published in The Barrister Magazine. Jack has a passion for both cars and motorsport, he has combined these obsessions by writing for DriveTribe, a motoring platform founded by the original Top Gear trio.'

Mark Linehan: Mark is a criminal defence solicitor and Higher Courts Advocate. He has over 30 years' experience acting for motorists in the magistrates' courts. He is a regular trial advocate and lectures practitioners and transport unions on practice and procedure in drink driving. He is a Director at Allen Hoole Ltd.

David Scutt: David was called to the Bar in 1989. His criminal practice includes homicide, other serious violent offending, firearms offending, serious sexual offending, drug-trafficking, human-trafficking, fraud and organised crime. David is an advocacy trainer, both in the UK and abroad (including the International Criminal Court in The Hague).

Caitlin Evans: Caitlin (call 2019) is a criminal practitioner who spent her first few years of practice in London before relocating to the West Country. Caitlin both prosecutes and defends, and is currently writing her Masters' thesis on the age of criminal responsibility.

Ray Tully KC: Ray is a specialist criminal practitioner and a former Head of the Crime Team in Guildhall Chambers. He has considerable experience in motor homicide cases. He grew up next to the car factory in Cowley, Oxford. His first car was an MG Midget with a leaky roof.

Peter Binder: Peter has over 30 years' experience as a defence advocate, mostly in London but now as an established member of the Guildhall Chambers Crime Team. In a previous life he worked in film and TV in Los Angeles, California, where he also managed a nightclub. His main pursuits outside the law are rock and roll music, buying and investing in wine, and the occasional bit of surfing. Last but far from least, he has had a life long devotion to the highs and lows of being a Manchester United fan.

Emily Evans: Emily qualified as a barrister and was called to the Bar in 2008. In 2011 she was admitted to the Roll of Solicitors attaining her higher rights in 2012. Emily currently practises as a Consultant Solicitor-Advocate. She also sits part-time as a Deputy District Judge (magistrates' court).

George Joseph: George was called to the bar in 2020, starting his criminal defence pupillage in September 2022 with Reeds Solicitors. Prior to pupillage, George worked as a Crown Court caseworker covering a wide array of serious offences including rape, attempted murder and conspiracy to supply drugs. Outside his life of crime George works as an on-call firefighter at his local station in Wiltshire.

Andrew Banks: Andrew is a solicitor advocate with higher rights in the criminal courts. His practice has included transport regulatory work since he qualified in 1996. He regularly appears as advocate before the Traffic Commissioners at Public Inquiries.

Table of Statutes

[All references are to paragraph numbers.]

Table of Statutory Instruments

[All references are to paragraph numbers.]

Table of Cases

[All references are to paragraph numbers.]

Part 1

Introduction

Chapter 1

Survival guide

Nick Lee

INTRODUCTION

1.1   The ambit of road traffic law is a wide one, ranging from some of the most innocuous and technical offences to some of the most serious and tragic. They are all, nonetheless, criminal offences, even if most result in fixed penalty notices, speed awareness courses, or other disposals which would not be available for more 'typical' crimes. Those offences that do reach court are therefore subject to criminal rules of evidence and the Criminal Procedure Rules. The prosecutor will be familiar with these rules, and any defendant will benefit from being represented by an advocate with experience in general criminal practice.

1.2   Notwithstanding this, road traffic law often feels like a distinct area of criminal law, and this chapter aims to assist prosecution and defence advocates in preparing their cases, particularly those offences at the less serious end of the spectrum, which resolve in the magistrates' court.

GENERAL PREPARATION

1.3   Although the most serious road traffic cases will be sent to the Crown Court for trial, or committed there for sentence, most will remain in the magistrates' court (unless later appealed). Familiarity with the workings of the magistrates' court therefore helps. On the day, find out if you are in front of a lay bench or a District Judge, be prepared to be patient while you wait to be called on, be polite to the usher and Legal Adviser (or risk finding yourself at the back of the queue), and do not keep the court waiting once it is ready to hear your case. If you are being prosecuted, and representing yourself, then speak to the usher, find out who the prosecutor is, and ask how the case against you is to be presented.

1.4   You may have been instructed late in the day by a defendant who has so far represented himself, in which case you will need to make sure you have a record of what has happened at earlier hearings, a copy of all correspondence and a complete set of the prosecution papers. If you need to make an application to the court for new directions, or to vacate trial, perhaps because there is a clear need for further enquiries (such as an expert report), do so sooner rather than later, asking for the case to be listed if needs be. If anything is missing from the papers, chase it down – unless (when defending) you take a tactical view that the missing material is actually a gap in the evidence which you should exploit.

1.5   Some road traffic cases require expert evidence to challenge the prosecution case (for example, whether a defendant with asthma could have provided a specimen of breath). Many defendants in the magistrates' court will be paying privately for representation, and their funds may not stretch to the costs of an expert report. It is worth considering if they are eligible for Legal Aid.

1.6   Cases involving vulnerable defendants, legal complexity, expert evidence, a risk of custody or someone losing their livelihood can pass the 'interests of justice' test and make Legal Aid available, provided the defendant also qualifies under the means test. A solicitors' firm which regularly undertakes criminal Legal Aid work will be able to advise the defendant further. If the defendant is paying privately and their case is successful, you should apply for a defence costs order to recoup at least some of the costs.

1.7   It goes without saying that you will need to read the papers carefully to identify and understand the issues in the case. Many chapters in this book offer practical advice in relation to the most frequently encountered offences, but an up-to-date edition of *Wilkinson's Road Traffic Offences* is indispensable for detailed legal analysis.

1.8   From the outset, you should ensure that you know and understand the elements of the offence, how the prosecution intends to prove them, what defences are available, the burden and standard of proof, what is actually in dispute, and which witnesses need to be warned. Do you need to make or respond to any legal applications? Would the case benefit from a defence case statement? This is not a requirement in the magistrates' court but often necessary if you seek further disclosure, and sometimes a useful way to 'set the agenda' by outlining the factual and legal issues in your terms.

1.9   If an element of the offence or a relevant legal concept has a degree of complexity, think about how you will explain it to a lay bench in a way which is advantageous to your argument. Should you prepare a written summary of the law for the bench to take with them when they retire? Even if you have served

4

applications or written submissions in advance, take printed copies with you to ensure the bench have your submissions to hand.

1.10 As with all criminal cases, many road traffic offences will resolve with a guilty plea, and your advocacy will be most needed when it comes to sentence. The more experience you have in other areas of criminal practice at opening or mitigating sentence, the better your advocacy in road traffic sentences will be.

1.11 If prosecuting, how will you introduce the facts, what are your submissions regarding the sentencing guidelines, and what other applications do you need to make? If defending, have a clear understanding of what you are seeking to achieve in mitigation, and take instructions on your client's finances to respond to any applications for compensation and/or costs. Your client will be asked to complete a means form, setting out his financial circumstances, on arrival at the court. If necessary, you should ask the usher to provide your client with the means form. Where relevant, you should also take instructions on whether the defendant wishes to attend a drink-drive rehabilitation course.

1.12 Whichever party you represent, you will need a working knowledge of the court's powers, any sentencing guidelines and, if applicable, the mechanics of disqualification (for example, is there a minimum mandatory disqualification, should one disqualification be imposed for a number of offences or should each offence attract its own disqualification, and should the disqualification be extended to reflect time in custody?).

1.13 Some of the more esoteric aspects of road traffic law relate to sentence. Subsequent chapters in this book deal with exceptional hardship applications and special reasons. If you are making or resisting these applications, ensure that you understand the law and think about how you will present or challenge the evidence in a way which is directed to those issues. If you are defending, consider whether prosecution witnesses need to be warned for a special reasons argument. What evidence do you need from the defendant to support the exceptional hardship application?

1.14 Every defendant convicted or sentenced in the magistrates' court has a right to appeal their conviction or sentence to the Crown Court. You may need to advise your client on the relative merits of appeal to the Crown Court or the High Court.

SOME COMMON CHALLENGES AND ISSUES

1.15 Defendants in road traffic cases may have no prior experience of criminal courts; it will be especially nerve-wracking for them and they will appreciate explanations about every step of the proceedings. A defendant with no previous convictions, a respectable job and a clean licence may feel aggrieved at the prospect of being disqualified and labelled a criminal for a momentary lapse in concentration. They may be worried about their job, house and family. They may have received dubious advice elsewhere about supposed loopholes or the strength of the evidence. If you have to give unwelcome advice or manage expectations, think about how you will do it.

1.16   Most magistrates are fair-minded, polite and reach a conclusion which is justified on the evidence. You may, however, sometimes feel yourself being regarded with suspicion by a lay bench which gives the impression of believing that a defendant who is represented in a road traffic case must be even more guilty (especially where drink driving is alleged). Hopefully your advocacy will change the atmosphere of the room but, if not, there is always the option of an appeal, if merited.

1.17   Many driving offences will not appear on a defendant's record of previous convictions. In some cases, you may wish to obtain the defendant's Driver Record Enquiry Report from the DVLA (often referred to as a 'DVLA record'). If you think this may be relevant, ask those instructing you to obtain the DVLA record well in advance of the case being heard. If you cannot do so, the Legal Adviser is often able to check how many points a defendant has on their licence.

1.18   The DVLA record itself is relatively easy to understand once you have it. The section titled 'Endorsement Details', usually on the second page, shows the previous offences endorsed on the defendant's licence. The offence code tells you what the previous offence was (there is a database of the codes on the gov. uk website: www.gov.uk/penalty-points-endorsements/endorsement-codes-and-penalty-points), and the date next to the offence code is the date of the offence. The court at which the defendant was convicted and sentenced is also given (by way of a code), as well as the dates of conviction and sentence. The record will show you what penalty was imposed, including any fine, penalty points or disqualification.

1.19   If you are defending, you will want to know in advance if your client is at risk of becoming a 'totter' (disqualified due to the accumulation of penalty points). If they cannot remember, they can access a record of their driving licence via the DVLA website. Failing that, those instructing you could try to obtain the DVLA record from the DVLA directly, or you could ask the Legal Adviser to assist once you reach court, although finding out that late will not leave you much time to prepare to mitigate a 'totting' disqualification.

1.20   If a defendant disputes the accuracy of the DVLA record, you may need to ask for an adjournment to enable the memorandum of conviction to be obtained from the magistrates' court which sentenced them in relation to the disputed offence. DVLA and PNC records can sometimes be incorrect; it is always worth checking basic details like the date of birth, especially if your client has a popular name.

1.21   The defendant should bring their driving licence to court. If it is going to be endorsed with penalty points or a disqualification, they will be asked to hand it over to the Legal Adviser. If endorsement only relates to penalty points, it will be returned soon after in the post. If the defendant has been disqualified, they will need to apply to the DVLA for a new licence using a form which will be sent to them 56 days before their disqualification ends. For defendants regarded as 'high risk' (including a defendant who has been disqualified for driving with excess alcohol for a second time in 10 years), the form will be sent 90 days before the end of the disqualification to allow time for a medical examination.

1.22   A defendant who is at risk of disqualification should not drive themselves to court. If disqualification is imposed, it is effective immediately and cannot be postponed, meaning that they will be left stranded and possibly facing further costs to recover their vehicle.

1.23   A disqualification can be suspended pending appeal. If you appeal conviction or sentence to the Crown Court and wish to request this, there is a box to tick on the appeal form (found on the Ministry of Justice website).

Chapter 2

Definitions of a vehicle and a road

Darren Burleigh

WHAT IS A VEHICLE?

2.1   The Road Traffic Act (RTA) 1988 regulates the use of vehicles on public roads and public places to which the public have access.

2.2   A 'vehicle' is defined as a 'carriage or conveyance of any kind used on land', in the *Concise Oxford Dictionary*, but is not defined as such in English law and may therefore cover anything that transports a person from A to B. Construction and use of vehicles, whether motor vehicles and trailers or pushbikes, is regulated by the Road Traffic Acts 1988 and 1991.

What is a motor vehicle?

2.3   There are various definitions of a 'motor vehicle' set out in section 185(1) of the RTA 1988, which covers everything from heavy locomotives to invalid carriages. In essence, the definition covers any mechanically propelled vehicle intended or adapted for use on roads. Vehicles which fall within this section that are used or kept on a public road must be registered with the DVLA, so that annual tax can be levied (Vehicle Excise and Registration Act 1994, s 1(1)).

Is the vehicle mechanically propelled?

2.4   The starting point for establishing whether a vehicle is a motor vehicle is to determine how it is propelled. Is it propelled mechanically by an engine, or is it self-propelled by a person? The meaning of 'mechanically propelled' is not defined in the legislation. It is therefore a matter of fact and degree to be determined by the court as to whether a vehicle was mechanically propelled at the relevant time. It requires vehicles to be propelled by some form of external power source and not just a person (eg a pushbike). The power source driving the engine or motor in a vehicle could be, for example, petrol, oil, steam or electricity.

2.5   The prosecution has to prove that it is a mechanically propelled vehicle although, if it looks like one, it is for the defendant to prove otherwise – eg if the engine has been stolen[1]. Temporary removal for repair of the engine will not remove the need for the vehicle to be taxed[2], but vehicles which are completely wrecked are no longer considered mechanically propelled[3]. It is a matter of fact and degree for the court to determine.

Is it constructed or modified so that it can be mechanically propelled?

2.6   To determine whether a vehicle is mechanically propelled, it might also be relevant to consider how it has been constructed or modified. In other words, to ask 'is the vehicle constructed so that it can be mechanically propelled?'.

Is the vehicle 'intended or adapted for use on roads'?

2.7   The courts have held that the question of whether a vehicle is 'intended or adapted for use on roads' should be judged by the 'reasonable person' standard[4]. Would a reasonable person think, from looking at the vehicle, that its general use included possible road use? It is for the prosecution to show that, having regard to the appearance of the vehicle and a potential user, the reasonable person would conclude that it could be used on the road.

2.8   The meaning of 'adapted' in this context is that the vehicle be 'fit and apt' for use on roads, not 'altered so as to be apt'[5]. Applying the 'reasonable person' test, a go-kart was found to be neither intended nor adapted for use on roads for the purposes of the RTA 1988[6]. Rather confusingly, a diesel dumper intended for use on a construction site only, not on a road, is considered to be a motor vehicle[7].

---

1   *Newberry v Simmonds* [1961] 2 QB 345, [1961] 2 All ER 318, 125 JP 409.
2   *Binks v Department of the Environment* (1975) 119 Sol Jo 304.
3   *Smart v Allen* [1963] 1 QB 291.
4   *Chief Constable of Avon and Somerset v Fleming* [1987] 1 All ER 318.
5   *Maddox v Storer* [1963] 1 QB 451.
6   *Burns v Currell* [1963] 2 QB 433.
7   *Daley v Hargreaves* [1961] 1 All ER 552.

2.9   However, application of the test more recently shows that 'intended' for use on roads does not mean that the vehicle must *only* be used on roads, merely whether driving on a road is one of its possible uses. Nor does it mean that the vehicle must be roadworthy. The courts have determined that a 'go-ped' (a motorised scooter) was intended or adapted for use on roads even though it did not comply with UK safety regulations and was not registered with the DVLA. The court held that, because the scooter was a vehicle (use on the road was 'within contemplation'), it therefore required a licence and insurance[8].

Application to e-scooters and other 'powered transporters'

2.10   *Saddington* (above) continues to be the authority applicable to the emerging transport devices collectively known as 'powered transporters' which include e-scooters, Segways, hoverboards, go-peds, powered unicycles and u-wheels. Such vehicles are considered 'motor vehicles' under the RTA 1988.

2.11   When *Saddington* was applied to e-scooters, the court found the 'City Mantis' e-scooter to be a motor vehicle within the meaning of the RTA 1988, regardless of the fact that its maximum speed at the time was 10 mph[9].

2.12   It should be borne in mind that only *rented* e-scooters or *rented* powered transporters are permitted for use on public roads in England and Wales. Those which are privately owned can only be used on private land. Those who ride private e-scooters on public roads do so unlawfully and would be committing offences such as driving without third party insurance. This law is widely flouted and, at the time of writing, is a challenge which the authorities are going to have to address in the near future. As of December 2021, there were estimated to be 750,000 privately owned e-scooters. Furthermore, there were reported to be 91 serious injuries and 9 fatalities in 2021, with the number of casualties having more than doubled since 2020[10].

2.13   Those who use the government-backed scheme for rental scooters or power transporters are subject to the same road traffic rules and regulations as any other person operating a vehicle. It is for this reason that the rental sector insists that, in order to register to rent a scooter, photographs of both front and back of the driving licence (full or provisional) are uploaded onto their system.

2.14   Anyone who rides a rental scooter when over the drink-drive limit is liable to lose their driving licence. Similarly, if they operate the vehicle in

8   *Chief Constable of North Yorkshire Police v Saddington* [2001] Crim LR 41.
9   *DPP v King* [2008] EWHC 447 (Admin).
10   Nicolas Hellen, Sunday Times, 9 January 2022.

contravention of its terms of use (for example, riding with a passenger), they could invalidate the insurance cover and thus be committing the offence of driving without third party insurance. Points can be added to a full driving licence as a result of misdemeanours in the use of a rented e-scooter, something which is often overlooked.

Application to e-bikes

2.15 E-bikes are generally considered to be 'electrically assisted pedal cycles' (EAPCs), which have their own regulatory framework. They are not motor vehicles, subject to the list below, and can be ridden by anyone who is aged 14 or over (RTA 1988, s 32).

2.16 It should be noted that, where any one of the following applies, the e-bike will be classified as a moped or motorcycle and thus the Act will apply:

(1)   electrical assistance is supplied to the e-bike thus making it capable of speeds of 15.5 mph or over (e-bikes are commonly limited to below this speed, so do not qualify as a moped, and need an adaptation to exceed it); or

(2)   it has a greater than 250W power output; or

(3)   it powers up without someone pedalling.

Trailers

2.17 Trailers are anything on wheels pulled by a motor vehicle, including a chicken shed with wheels attached! They are deemed to be part of the vehicle, as set out in section 186(2) of the RTA 1988[11].

WHAT IS A ROAD?

2.18 Section 142 (General interpretation of Act) of the Road Traffic Regulation Act 1984 states:

> '"road" – (a) in England and Wales, means any length of highway or of any other road to which the public has access, and includes bridges over which a road passes, and (b) in Scotland, has the same meaning as in the Roads (Scotland) Act 1984.'

---

11   *Garner v Burr* [1951] 1 KB 31.

2.19   This may seem obvious but, for the purpose of a prosecution under the various Road Traffic Acts, the alleged offence must have taken place on a road. The definition of a road therefore matters. It is, of course, for the prosecution to prove that a road is one to which the Act applies and that it is a public space. Section 192(1) of the RTA 1988 states that a road includes (but importantly, is not limited to) *any highway and any other road to which the public has access* and includes bridges over which a road passes.

2.20   Mechanically propelled vehicles can only be driven on roads, and are specifically prohibited from driving upon footpaths, bridleways and restricted byways or moorland unless given permission by the landowner. There is an exception for parking off-road, though that extends to no more than 15 yards from the road (RTA 1988, s 34(1)).

Is it a highway?

2.21   Whether or not a highway exists depends on whether the general public has access to the area of land in question. Megarry and Wade, *The Law of Real Property* (5th edn, 1984), puts it in rather tortuous language:

> 'The land over which a public right of way exists is known as a highway; and although most highways have been made up into roads, and most easements of way exist over footpaths, the presence or absence of a made road has nothing to do with the distinction. There may be a highway over a footpath, while a well-made road may be subject only to an easement of way or may exist only for the landowner's benefit and be subject to no easement at all.'

Is the highway a road?

2.22   Ask: 'does the physical character and the function which the space in question serves make it a road for the purposes of the Act?'. The physical character of a road is a question of fact. Roads ought to have a definitive route and fairly obvious sides and edges. However, whilst some roads may be constructed so the sides are clearly ascertainable, others may simply have developed by the repeated passage of traffic over the same land. As for a defined start and finish, a road can of course be continuous or come to a dead end, as it does with a cul-de-sac.

A road should lead from one place to another, allowing its users to move conveniently between the points to and from which it leads.

13

Do the public have access?

2.23   If the physical character of a road cannot be defined in fact, then the next question to consider is whether the public have access to it. A road is a carriageway to which the public have access – that is, the legal right to pass and re-pass. The term 'public' refers to the general public, as distinguishable from persons who belong to a special class of people and/or who have a personal reason to access the road, such as postmen, milkmen or the police. Public access is a matter of fact and degree, and the onus is on the prosecution to provide evidence as to the degree to which the public has access[12].

2.24   A road, for the purposes of the RTA 1988, will be deemed as such if, at the time of an alleged offence, the public had access to it even if, at other times, access to the public is not apparent or if the road is private, for example, if it is situated on a private farm, and if 'the public generally did have access to the private road in question without objection'[13]. The principal use and ownership of a road does not matter if the public has access to it; it is the degree to which they have access that matters[14].

Is it 'any other road to which the public have access'?

2.25   Pavements, grass verges and slip roads or filter lanes are generally considered to form a part of a road and are accessed by the general public. Therefore, as a whole they constitute a road for the purposes of the Act. When these are maintained at public expense, even if they are in part privately owned, they will still be deemed to be part of a road and therefore fall under the Act.

2.26   Footpaths, usually defined as somewhere that the public has the right of way by foot only, might be deemed to be a road if the criteria for being a highway are met. Thus, a conviction for riding a motorcycle on a five-foot wide public footpath, impassable to motor cars, was upheld because the footpath was deemed in these circumstances to be a highway[15]. By contrast, the term 'footway' is usually used to denote a right of way on foot only – eg a pavement.

2.27   A square, such as Trafalgar Square, or a marketplace can be deemed to be roads, depending on the precise circumstances of each case. It is for the justices to decide whether any given location is a road[16]. Similarly, a route with

---

12   *Hallett v DPP* [2011] EWHC 488 (Admin).
13   *Harrison v Hill* 1932 JC 13.
14   *Price v DPP* [1990] RTR 413.
15   *Lang v Hindhaugh* [1986] RTR 271.
16   *Sadiku v DPP* [2000] RTR 155.

road markings and signage, used by members of the public to gain access to a beach via the private road through a caravan park, is a road[17].

2.28   However, the Act will not apply to roads to which the public do not have the right to access. A road which is contained within the fenced boundaries of a factory premises, or a road to a shipping dock, will not constitute a road, because it would only be accessible to people with special access passes or codes[18]. The general principle is that a private road, used only by residents and their guests, does not qualify as a public road. This would include a road leading to a housing estate, used by residents and their visitors with permission from the Council. In such a case, the prosecutor would need to establish that the general public had access[19].

If it is not a road, is it a 'public place'?

2.29   If the space in question is not capable of being a road, it may be necessary to determine whether it is a 'public place'. This requires it to be accessible and used by the general public.

In cases concerning private land, the critical distinction is between private land to which the public have access at the time in question, and private land which is closed to the public at the material time or is only open to a special class of people. Where a company car park was used by members of the public, the magistrates were able to determine that it was a public place for the purposes of a drink-driving offence[20].

Car parks

2.30   It is up to the magistrates to determine as a matter of fact whether a particular car park is a road[21], but a car park will be deemed to be a 'public place' if, for example, it is adjoining a main road and in use by the public[22]. A pub car park is a public place during the pub's licensing hours, but outside of these hours, and if reserved for patrons only, it will not be[23].

However, if the pub has a pay and display car park which operates outside of licensing hours for the benefit of the general public, it will be a public place during parking hours.

---

17   *Barrett v DPP* [2009] EWHC 423 (Admin).
18   *Buchanan v Motor Insurers Bureau* [1955] 1 All ER 607.
19   *Deacon v AT* [1976] RTR 244.
20   *Filmer v DPP* [2006] EWHC 3450 (Admin).
21   *Griffin v Squires* [1958] 3 All ER 468.
22   *May v DPP* [2005] EWHC 1280 (Admin).
23   *Sandy v Martin* [1974] Crim LR 258.

2.31   A car park is not a public place if it is specifically for the use of company staff, customers and other visitors, save in cases where there is evidence of actual use by the general public. The mere fact that the car park has no barrier preventing the public from accessing it is not conclusive evidence of it being a public place[24].

Lawyers beware

2.32   Road traffic cases are generally dealt with by courts local to the area in question. This means that the magistrates' bench may have specific local knowledge. It might be necessary to remind the tribunal of the advice from the Divisional Court in *Bowman v DPP* [1991] RTR 263 (where a multi-storey car park without a barrier was held to be a 'public place' for the purposes of drink-driving) that, if they are to rely upon their local knowledge in consideration of the case, the court should say so in open court, to give the lawyers an opportunity to comment.

---

24   *Spence* [1999] RTR 353.

Part 2

Procedure

Chapter 3

'How to be legal'

Grace Flynn

3.1   Passing a driving test is a licence to the freedom of the road and a cause for celebration. However, excitement aside, driving also brings with it a significant number of practical responsibilities and administrative tasks that, if overlooked, will land a driver in hot legal water.

STANDARD REQUIREMENTS

3.2   As a basic guide to the fundamental requirements, drivers need to ensure that they have:

(i)   a licence for the correct category of vehicle (updated with any change of address);

(ii)   a valid insurance policy (minimum third-party cover);

(iii)   registered the vehicle with the DVLA;

(iv)   updated the logbook (V5C);

(v)   a valid MOT certificate;

(vi)   paid the required vehicle tax; and

(vii)   met any eyesight/health requirements and reported any problems to the DVLA.

3.3   As this chapter will illustrate, missing one of the above can often lead to a problem with one of the other requirements. For example, driving without a licence will invalidate an insurance policy. It is because of this that a defendant will often face multiple driving charges, all stemming from the same incident.

3.4   People with very little experience of the criminal justice system often encounter it for the first time as a result of failing to meet all of their obligations

and, of course, speeding. Criminologists have studied the phenomenon of those who consider themselves 'law abiding' citizens being outraged at falling foul of road traffic offences (which are frequently offences of strict liability).

3.5 Helen Wells' study, *The Fast and The Furious: Drivers, Speed Cameras and Control in a Risk Society (Human Factors in Road and Rail Transport)*[1], considers how enraged many drivers are at the inability to argue with a human being as the face of law enforcement. Simply put, you cannot charm a speed camera out of a ticket. Equally, automatic number plate recognition (ANPR) cameras scan number plates to identify who is driving without having paid their vehicle tax, and a fine is automatically issued as a result. There is no opportunity to debate with machinery, and there are rarely defences to any of the offences which stem from failing to meet all of your obligations.

3.6 It is, of course, important to keep up to date with any changes in the law, and these tend to be communicated in public information campaigns. There has, for example, been recent publicity concerning incoming changes to strengthen the existing laws against using a hand-held mobile phone whilst driving, and an updated Highway Code has transformed the responsibilities of drivers in relation to other road users.

THE DRIVING TEST – THEORY AND PRACTICAL

3.7 A keen learner driver can order their provisional licence aged 15 years and 9 months old but will have to wait to take the practical test at 17. A theory test must be passed before the practical driving test is taken. Theory test pass certificates are valid for two years, and the test must be retaken if they expire before the practical takes place.

3.8 Bear in mind that a manual driving licence holder is also 'automatically' qualified to drive an automatic vehicle. However, it does not work the other way around. An automatic licence holder needs to upgrade their licence to be covered to drive a manual.

3.9 Different licences are required for a wide range of vehicles on the road. Drivers must ensure that they are aware of the requirements for their specific vehicle and ensure they have taken the relevant theory test. A standard manual car licence does *not* allow a driver to drive the following categories, many of which require significant additional driving skills:

- motorbike (categories A1, A2 and A);

1   Published by CRC Press (1st edition, 2011).

- moped (category P or AM);

- medium-sized vehicles (category C1);

- large vehicles and lorries (category C);

- minibus (category D1);

- bus (category D);

- agricultural tractor (category F);

- other specialist vehicles (categories G, H and K);

- quad bikes (category B1); and

- motor tricycle (categories A and A1).

3.10   Failing to ensure that you have met all of the above is an oversight that can lead a driver to face penalties, typically those listed below.

3.11   The vast majority are offences of strict liability and therefore there is no defence in law, but there are some rare exceptions. Penalties tend to be financial and penalty point-based, and there is of course the risk of disqualification for some.

OFFENCES

Driving otherwise than in accordance with a licence (RTA 1988, s 87)

3.12   Driving without a licence, or with the wrong type of licence, is the summary-only offence of 'driving otherwise than in accordance with a licence'. It is also an offence to allow someone to drive your vehicle, knowing that they do not have the appropriate licence to do so. It is a significant aggravating feature to drive a vehicle having never had a licence to do so.

The penalty is 3 to 6 points plus a fine.

Using a vehicle uninsured against third party risks (RTA 1988, s 143)

3.13   Drivers must be covered by an insurance policy. The minimum for standard cars is third party cover, which ensures that third parties who you collide with are covered, but repairs to your own vehicle, or injury to yourself, will not be. The policy must be from an authorised insurer and insure against death or injury to any person, or damage to property 'caused by, or arising out of, the use of a vehicle on a road in Great Britain'[2].

The maximum penalty is 6 to 8 points or disqualification plus a fine.

3.14   As with driving without a licence, it is an offence to allow someone else to drive your vehicle knowing that they are not insured[3]. Whilst rarely charged, it is notable that even an honest, but mistaken, belief that someone is insured is no defence[4]. The first question you should ask when you are about to get behind the wheel of someone else's car is not 'where are the controls', but 'am I insured?'.

3.15   Crucially, insurance policies can be invalidated by a failure to ensure that all other requirements are met. For example, a driver who does not hold a valid licence cannot, by definition, be covered by any insurance policy.

3.16   If an insurance policy is void and the driver continues to drive without rectifying the situation, they are driving without insurance. It is as if the policy never existed from the start, and no claims will be allowed. Even driving for an hour without insurance is an offence.

3.17   The following are examples of matters that can invalidate insurance:

(i)   no MOT;

(ii)   wrong type of licence for the category of vehicle;

(iii)   failing to disclose any relevant health conditions or eyesight issues;

(iv)   not keeping your main address up to date (a student, having registered their car at their home address, needs to update the insurer if they take their car with them away to university and are based there the majority of the time); and

(v)   'fronting' (a tactic when the policyholder (mum or dad) misleads the insurance provider by putting a less-experienced driver (19-year-old son) down as a named additional driver in order to obtain lower premiums; in reality, the less-experienced driver is the main driver). Should the insurer discover this, they could void the policy and class this as insurance fraud.

3.18   Police have the power to seize and destroy vehicles which are driven without insurance. It has been reported that, in 2020, over 75,000 cars were impounded for having no insurance; in February 2020, the Motor Insurance Bureau confirmed that, since 2005, two million uninsured vehicles had been seized. Many of these cars are later destroyed by the police unless the owner

---

2   RTA 1988, s 145.
3   RTA 1988, s 143(1)(b).
4   *Lloyd-Wolper v Moore* [2004] EWCA Civ 766, [2004] RTR 30.

comes forward to prove that they now have insurance and pays a fine and the costs of storage.

3.19   Whilst most situations of driving without insurance are clear cut on the facts, there is a statutory defence for a very specific situation. Under section 143(3) of the RTA 1988, an employee who drives their employer's vehicle in the course of their work, unaware that there was no insurance in place, has a defence.

Section 143(3) of the RTA 1988

3.20

'A person charged with using a motor vehicle in contravention of this section shall not be convicted if he proves—

(a)   that the vehicle did not belong to him and was not in his possession under a contract of hiring or of loan,

(b)   that he was using the vehicle in the course of his employment, and

(c)   that he neither knew nor had reason to believe that there was not in force in relation to the vehicle such a policy of insurance as is mentioned in subsection (1) above.'

3.21   The penalty for driving without insurance can be a fixed penalty (currently set at £300) and 6 to 8 penalty points, an unlimited fine and the potential for a driving disqualification order. Disqualification is discretionary, but there is an obligatory endorsement with between 6 and 8 penalty points.

No Obligatory Test Certificate (MOT) (RTA 1988, s 47)

3.22   First introduced in 1960, the 'MOT' (Ministry of Transport) test applies to the majority of vehicles which are over three years old. However, vehicles with more than eight seats (excluding the driver's seat, typically people carriers/minibuses), taxis and ambulances are required to pass an MOT after their first year. It is a legal requirement to ensure that the vehicle is booked in for and passes an annual check of roadworthiness. Driving a vehicle without an MOT will lead to a fine and can invalidate an insurance policy.

3.23   It is possible to raise a very specific defence. The driver can be driving without an MOT if they can prove that they were taking their vehicle to their MOT test appointment at the time at which they were stopped. A driver would need to provide proof of the appointment and potentially a witness from the test centre to confirm this.

3.24 The penalty is a fine up to £1,000.

No tax (Vehicle Excise and Registration Act 1994, s 29 and Sch 2A, and Vehicle Excise Duty (Immobilisation, Removal and Disposal of Vehicles) Regulations 1997)

3.25 Another annual requirement is to pay the appropriate vehicle tax or, if not using the vehicle, to complete a Statutory Off-Road Notification (SORN)[5]. It used to be the case that a tax disc, displayed in the front of the car, was the requirement to prove that you were up to date with your payments. However, the days of putting a Guinness bottle label in the window as a tax disc lookalike are long gone. Vehicle tax and SORNs are now monitored electronically and the odds of being caught out are extremely high. ANPR cameras are used to scan registrations and check them against the DVLA's database.

3.26 If you fail to pay your tax, you face a financial penalty. The DVLA has the right to clamp the vehicle until it is paid. Usually an out-of-court settlement (OCS) letter is first issued, with a fine of £30 plus one and a half times the vehicle tax owed. If not paid, the offence may be sent to the magistrates' court where the penalty will be up to £1,000 or five times the amount of tax due (whichever is the greater). Paying the OCS and arranging an MOT as soon as possible, to avoid another letter, is advisable.

3.27 Electric cars (but not hybrid vehicles) are not currently subject to road tax, but this will change in 2025.

No tax – driving with a SORN in force

3.28 Having completed a SORN means that you do not need to pay tax. The driver is declaring that the vehicle is not being driven on public roads and is therefore exempt. Generally, it is being kept off the road (in a garage, on a drive, or on private land). If your vehicle is not declared as SORN, you must ensure the tax is paid for. A SORN car cannot be driven on public roads until the notification is cancelled (it does not, as it used to, lapse after a set period of time).

3.29 Driving a car on a public road when it is declared as SORN is an offence with heavier financial penalties than driving without tax. Again, an OCS letter is issued. If the letter is ignored, the matter will proceed to the magistrates' court

5   Apply online or complete form V890.

where the penalty is a fine of up to £2,500 or five times the amount of tax due (whichever is the greater).

3.30   As with driving without an MOT certificate, there is a possible (and very specific) defence, that you are only driving your SORN declared vehicle to and from a pre-booked MOT appointment.

Lighting

3.31   Even if your vehicle has a valid MOT, driving without the appropriate lights functioning on your vehicle can also lead to penalties. It is your responsibility to check your vehicle and be aware of, and swiftly rectify, any defects, to avoid falling foul of the Highway Code and be considered at fault in any collision.

3.32   Faulty lighting has long been a textbook excuse for the police to stop a vehicle and provide justification for conducting a breath test or a search of the vehicle or driver. It is easily avoided!

Duty of driver to stop, report accident and give information or documents (RTA 1988, s 170)

3.33   A driver must stop at the scene of an accident if a person is injured or another person's vehicle, animal or property is damaged. An animal is defined as: 'a horse, cattle, ass, mule, sheep, pig, goat or dog'[6]. Perhaps controversially, a cat is not included in this list.

3.34   Leaving the scene of an accident is commonly described as a 'hit and run'. It is taken extremely seriously by the courts and, indeed, by society. The penalties can be severe and include a possible prison sentence of up to six months in the most extreme cases.

3.35   Failure to stop is an offence under section 170(2), and failure to report an accident where required to do so is an offence under section 170(3). Following an accident, information must be exchanged with the other driver (name, vehicle registration and insurance details) and anyone who has reasonable grounds to ask for them. If you are unable to provide these details (for example, if there is nobody else present at the scene), the accident must be reported to the police 'as soon as reasonably practicable and, in any case, within twenty-four hours'[7]. This

---

6   RTA 1988, s 170(8).
7   RTA 1988, s 170(6)(b).

includes producing a valid insurance certificate if required. A driver who does stop but refuses to provide their details (or fails to do so at a police station within 24 hours) is guilty of an offence.

3.36 When it comes to sentencing for 'failing to stop', factors of higher culpability include:

(i) an offence committed in circumstances where a request for a sample of breath, blood or urine would have been made if the offender had stopped;

(ii) an offence committed by an offender seeking to avoid arrest for another offence;

(iii) an offender knew or suspected that personal injury was caused and/or left an injured party at the scene; and

(iv) giving false details.

3.37 Disqualification for this offence is discretionary, but endorsement of the licence, with five to ten penalty points, is obligatory. It is also possible for forfeiture of the vehicle to be ordered.

Failure to provide details of identity of driver (RTA 1988, s 172)

3.38 Section 172 of the RTA 1988 states that it is an offence not to provide details of the driver of a vehicle when requested to do so by a Notice of Intended Prosecution (NIP). This is a common problem in speeding cases, often resulting in convictions in the magistrates' court which are then appealed in the Crown Court.

3.39 Typically, when a camera records a breach of the speed limit, the registered keeper is sent an NIP to the address held by the DVLA – a key reason why it is important to ensure that the address is correct and up to date. A response must be provided within 28 days; if someone other than the registered keeper was driving, that driver's details must be given so that a fresh NIP is sent to that person.

3.40 If no response is received, a prosecution may be commenced for failing to provide the requested information. Whilst the initial offence was the speeding, this charge drops away when proceedings are started and only the failure to provide information is prosecuted. In these circumstances, a speeding fine is preferable to the penalty for failing to provide information – though that is not a choice that the driver can make. Failure to provide information is the preferred charge.

3.41   Often these prosecutions occur because the NIP was not received (even if the correct address is used, post can sometimes go astray – for example, in a large block of flats with inadequate post boxes) and, if a conviction follows because the registered keeper was unaware of the summons, the automatic result is a conviction and six mandatory points on the driving licence.

3.42   It is often the case that the registered keeper first becomes aware of the offence when they are told that they have a conviction and six points on their licence, together with a large fine (if the defendant has not attended because they were not aware of the summons, the magistrates have no information about means and often impose high fines). The only route is appeal to the Crown Court where the appellant will have to give evidence about why they did not know about the summons.

3.43   A defence is provided by section 172(4) of the RTA 1988 if the registered keeper 'did not know and could not with reasonable diligence have ascertained who the driver of the vehicle was'. However, it is not sufficient to say that two people shared the driving and you cannot remember who was driving at the point when the speeding took place. This is an area of law which has resulted in an immense body of case law, far too great for this book to deal with; but, in general terms, it is clear that the rules are strictly enforced. The expectation will be that, even in a family where three or four people share one car, it should be known who was driving on any given day.

3.44   Companies as well as individuals can be convicted of an offence under section 172 of the RTA 1988. Such a situation can arise where the vehicle caught speeding is a company car. If the registered keeper of the vehicle is the company, the NIP will be sent to the company address in the first instance. If convicted, the company will receive a fine, but penalty points cannot be imposed on a company.

POSSESSION OF A FALSE DRIVING LICENCE

3.45   There are two offences under the Identity Documents Act 2010:

- section 4 (Possession of false identity documents etc with improper intention); and

- section 6 (Possession of false identity documents etc without reasonable excuse).

3.46   Section 4 of the Identity Documents Act 2010 relates to someone using a false licence in order to commit further offences or to find out personal information about an individual. The maximum sentence is 10 years' imprisonment.

3.47   Possession of a false licence, or using another person's licence and passing it off as your own, is an offence under section 6 of the Identity Documents Act 2010. The maximum sentence is two years on indictment and/or a fine. There is a defence of reasonable excuse, which is most commonly seen in cases of immigration fraud and victims of human trafficking and modern slavery.

3.48   This chapter is not intended to alarm but to highlight the responsibilities that all drivers face and how staying on top of administrative tasks is crucial. Setting a reminder on a phone or calendar when your insurance is due for renewal, making sure you book in your MOT in advance of its expiration date, and ensuring that your address is up to date with the DVLA when you move house are ways to avoid these simple tasks being overlooked in our busy lives. There are, of course, more serious offences in this chapter, such as fraud and failing to report an accident, which are not offences that someone could fall foul of due to poor organisation and, as a result, they are viewed harshly by the courts.

Chapter 4

Licences

Alistair Haggerty

4.1   Driving licences are a complicated subject, governed by a range of different legislative provisions. The most important are the Motor Vehicles (Driving Licences) Regulations 1999 ('the 1999 Regulations') and the Motor Vehicles (Driving Licences) (Amendment) Regulations 2012. A complete list of the categories of vehicle licence is outlined in Schedule 2 to the 1999 Regulations.

4.2   The standard driving licence – and the one most commonly encountered by the courts – is a category B licence, which enables the holder to drive motor cars and small goods vehicles. A category B licence is also sufficient to drive vehicles in categories F (agricultural or forestry tractors), K (ride-on lawnmowers) and P (mopeds). However, separate tests must be passed by those with a category B licence before holders are able to drive medium-sized goods vehicles and buses.

LEARNER DRIVERS

4.3   There are two parts to the driving test (the theory test and the practical test) for those who wish to obtain a full driving licence. Both parts need to be passed before a full licence can be obtained. The requirement to pass a two-stage test applies in relation to cars (category B licence) and those intending to drive medium-sized and large goods and passenger-carrying vehicles. Prior to passing the test, the driver will need to hold a provisional licence.

4.4   A provisional licence holder must, when driving a vehicle subject to the provisional licence, be under the supervision of a qualified driver and must display a 'distinguishing mark' (which, in most cases, will be 'L' plates). There are legal obligations for a qualified driver who supervises a learner driver. They are, for example, under a duty to do whatever is reasonably expected to prevent the learner driver from acting carelessly or in a manner likely to cause danger to others[1]. The supervisor must also be present with the learner driver in or on the vehicle. Under regulation 17 of the 1999 Regulations, a driver supervising a provisional licence holder driving passenger-carrying or goods vehicles must have held the necessary licence for a period of three years. Where an offence is committed by the provisional licence holder when driving the vehicle (for example, driving with excess alcohol), the supervisor may also be convicted of aiding and abetting the main offence if they had knowledge of the illegality.

4.5   Upon the successful completion of the driving test, the driver is issued with a licence. This is granted until the holder turns 70 (in the absence of any disease or disability), albeit the licence has to be re-issued every ten years to ensure the accuracy of the personal information and photograph. For those over 70 years of age, the licence is renewable every three years.

NEW DRIVERS

4.6   Newly qualified drivers (ie those who pass their practical and theory test) have a two-year probationary period. The Road Traffic (New Drivers) Act 1995 stipulates that drivers who accrue six penalty points on their licence within two years of passing their first driving test have their full licence revoked until they pass a further test. Under section 5 of the 1995 Act, the new driver's entitlement to drive is restored in cases where there is an appeal pending against the court decision to impose penalty points. Unsurprisingly, if the appeal fails, the restoration of the licence ends.

REQUIREMENT TO PRODUCE DRIVING LICENCE

4.7   Under section 164 of the Road Traffic Act 1988 ('RTA 1988'), the police have the power to demand that you produce your driving licence. This power arises in circumstances where the police have reasonable cause to believe that you have committed a driving offence, have been involved in an accident, or were supervising a learner driver involved in an offence or accident. However, they can simply demand that you produce your licence if you are driving a car when they stop you.

4.8   Failure to produce your driving licence when required is an offence. However, the offence does not arise if, within seven days, you produce your driving licence in person at a police station or produce it in person as soon as is reasonably practicable.

---

1   *Rubie v Faulkner* [1940] 1 All ER 285.

DISEASE OR DISABILITY

4.9   Under section 92 of the RTA 1988, an application for a driving licence must include a declaration by the applicant stating whether they are suffering from, or have during the prescribed period suffered from, a relevant disability or prospective disability. A relevant disability includes any disability which is likely to cause the driving of a vehicle to be a source of danger to the public. As the term suggests, prospective disability is one which, due to its intermittent or progressive nature, may become a relevant disability in the course of time.

4.10   If it appears to the Secretary of State that the applicant is suffering from a relevant disability, they must, subject to some caveats, refuse to grant the driving licence. The caveats include the applicant having passed their test since the time of the disability arising and that disability not having become more acute.

4.11   Section 92(10) of the RTA 1988 stipulates that a person who holds a driving licence is guilty of an offence if the declaration made as to physical fitness in the application on which the licence was granted was one which they knew to be false.

4.12   Under section 93 of the RTA 1988, the Secretary of State may revoke a driving licence. In order to do so, two criteria need to be satisfied. First, that the licence holder is suffering from a relevant disability and, second, that the Secretary of State would have been required, by virtue of section 92, to refuse an application for the licence made at that time. If satisfied that the licence should be revoked, the Secretary of State will serve notice revoking the licence with effect from a date specified. The procedure is the same in circumstances where the licence holder is suffering from a prospective disability. Under section 93(3), a person whose licence is revoked must surrender their licence 'forthwith after the revocation'. Failure to do so, without reasonable excuse, is an offence.

4.13   Section 94 of the RTA 1988 imposes a duty of disclosure upon driving licence holders. This provision means that the licence holder is required to inform the relevant authorities of any relevant or prospective disability, which had not been disclosed at the time of making the licence application. This duty extends to situations in which a previously disclosed disability has become more acute since the licence was granted. Nevertheless, the duty does not arise where the licence holder has reasonable grounds for believing that the duration of the disability will not extend beyond a period of three months from the date of discovery.

4.14   Regulation 71 of the 1999 Regulations outlines the diseases and disabilities which may justify the refusal of a driving licence. These are:

31

(i)   epilepsy;

(ii)   severe mental disorder;

(iii) liability to sudden attacks of disabling giddiness or fainting; and

(iv)   persistent misuse of drugs or alcohol, whether or not such misuse amounts to dependency.

4.15   The provisions relating to medical fitness differ according to the type of vehicle that one is licensed to drive. Regulation 73 of the 1999 Regulations sets out the stricter standards for those licensed to drive medium-sized and large goods vehicles, including stricter eye tests. There are also separate provisions for those with diabetes under this regulation. Drivers who have diabetes treated with insulin are not barred from obtaining a licence, provided that they do not have impaired awareness, they have been without more than one severe hypoglycaemic attack in a year, and they meet the conditions set out in regulation 73(10) of the 1999 Regulations. These requirements are, again, stricter for those who wish to be licensed to drive larger goods vehicles.

4.16   There are specific provisions for those classified as problem drinkers which mean that their licences may not be automatically returned at the expiry of a disqualification period. Regulation 74 of the 1999 Regulations allows the DVLA to regulate the return of a licence if the applicant falls into one of the following three categories:

(i)   Those disqualified for driving with an alcohol level of over 200mg in 100ml of blood, 87.5mg in 100ml of breath, or 267.5mg in 100ml of urine.

(ii)   Those disqualified twice for drink driving offences within a ten-year period.

(iii) Those disqualified for refusing to supply a specimen for analysis.

4.17   After a relevant conviction, the DVLA will advise the individual that consideration will be given as to whether the conviction indicates a medical disability. Ninety days before the end of the disqualification, the DVLA will arrange for a medical examination to take place with a DVLA doctor to prove fitness to drive.

APPEAL

4.18   Section 100 of the RTA 1988 provides a right of appeal against the refusal or revocation of a licence or a decision to grant a full licence for three years or less (under section 99(1)(b)). However, where a licence has been refused because of defective eyesight which was disclosed by the applicant in their application, they cannot appeal under section 100[2]. Similarly, the court will not

---

2   *R v Cumberland JJ ex p Hepworth* (1931) 95 JP 206.

entertain an application where an examiner has failed the applicant in a driving test. The burden is on the appellant to establish that they are entitled to a licence.

LICENCE OFFENCES

Driving otherwise than in accordance with a licence

4.19   According to section 87(1) of the RTA 1988, it is an offence for a person to drive on a road a vehicle of any class otherwise than in accordance with the licence required. Once the prosecution proves that the vehicle was driven on a road, it is for the defendant to prove, on the balance of probabilities, that they had the required licence[3].

4.20   Under section 87(2) of the RTA 1988, it is an offence to cause or permit another person to drive otherwise than in accordance with the necessary licence. Although the law is not settled on this point, this provision appears to impose a duty upon employers to ensure that those they employ to drive vehicles are covered by the appropriate licence. An offence under section 87 is punishable with a fine and up to six penalty points.

Driving whilst disqualified

4.21   Under section 103 of the RTA 1988, it is an offence for a disqualified driver to obtain a licence or drive a vehicle on the road. It is a serious offence, carrying up to six months' imprisonment, and is one of strict liability. It is for the prosecution to prove that the driver was disqualified and driving on the road at the relevant time. Once this is established, there is very little available by way of a defence. However, the Court of Appeal has held that, in very limited situations, a defence of necessity could arise from duress of circumstances[4].

4.22   Showing that a driver is disqualified requires strict proof. It was held that this can be done by admission, by fingerprints, or by evidence from a person present in court at the time of conviction to identify the defendant[5]. In subsequent cases, the court has observed that there is no exhaustive list of methods of proof[6].

4.23   Before resuming driving, a disqualified driver will need to apply for a new licence, as the previous licence is treated as revoked.

3   *John v Humphreys* [1955] 1 All ER 793.
4   *R v Martin* [1989] RTR 63.
5   *R v Derwentside JJ ex parte Heaviside* [1996] RTR 384.
6   *R v Derwentside Magistrates' Court ex parte Swift; R v Sunderland Magistrates' Court ex parte Bate* [1997] RTR 89.

Chapter 5

Basic procedure

Mandla Ndovlu

5.1 The process in road traffic offences mirrors the procedure in other criminal offences. Nevertheless, and perhaps unsurprisingly, there are a few quirks which are addressed in this chapter.

GETTING TO COURT

5.2 Prosecutors can begin criminal proceedings for any offence in two ways:

(1) Issue of a written charge and requisition, giving the time and date for a first hearing at the magistrates' court, or a 'single justice procedure notice', used in simple (eg speeding) cases where the defendant is asked to indicate whether they are intending to plead guilty, and, if so, whether the case can be heard in their absence. A magistrate will decide the case without the defendant's input if there is no response to the notice within 21 days.

(2) Issue of a summons; this is a judicial function and there are set requirements (it must be in time, an offence known to law, etc).

5.3 The Road Traffic Offenders Act 1988 (RTOA 1988) sets out further conditions which must be adhered to in cases which relate to:

- dangerous/careless driving;
- dangerous/careless bike riding;
- failing to comply with traffic directions,
- leaving a vehicle in a dangerous position; or
- aiding and abetting any of the above [a full list can be found at RTOA 1988, Sch 1]; or
- speeding (RTOA 1988, Sch 1, para 1A).

5.4   In any of these cases, the defendant must have been warned about the possibility of prosecution. Although, in theory, the warning can be verbal, it is normally done via a Notice of Intended Prosecution (NIP), or service of a summons within 14 days of the offence. The NIP is sent to the registered keeper of the vehicle. If the registered keeper was not the driver at the relevant time, it is their responsibility to say who was the driver at the time of the alleged offence.

5.5   It should be noted that this 'warning' is not required for cases of manslaughter or death by dangerous driving. An exemption applies under section 2(1) of the RTOA 1988 where an accident has occurred; although, in fact, it is normal practice for the NIP to be served.

5.6   The time limits for issuing prosecutions are rigid. Whether you are prosecuting or defending, it is important to check that this has been complied with upon receiving the brief. All 'summary only' offences must be in court no later than six months from the date when the prosecutor knew there was sufficient evidence to warrant the proceedings. No prosecution can be brought to court more than three years after the commission of any offence. There is a great deal of complex case law which needs to be examined carefully if there is any doubt as to the legitimacy of the issuing of proceedings. It is for the defence to prove that the requirements have not been fulfilled, and it is not for the Crown to prove that they have been complied with.

5.7   The court will presume a notice to have been correctly served if it was sent by registered post or recorded delivery service and addressed to the defendant at their last known address. It does not matter if the notice is returned as undelivered or was, for any other reason, not received; but it must, in general, have been posted to reach the intended recipient within the time limit.

THE COURT PROCESS

5.8   The defendant will make their first appearance in the magistrates' court. The court will check they have the right person and read out the offences they are accused of committing. The defendant will then be asked how they intend to plead: guilty or not guilty.

5.9   A 'guilty' plea will lead straight to sentencing, which will either take place in the magistrates' court or be sent to the Crown Court if the magistrates' sentencing powers are deemed insufficient.

5.10   The case will proceed to trial if the defendant enters a 'not guilty' plea in the magistrates' court. This can occur in the magistrates' court if the offence is 'summary only' or 'either-way'. In the latter case, the defendant can choose to have their case heard in either the Crown Court or magistrates' court, or the magistrates may decline jurisdiction (see Chapter 6 for more details).

5.11 A trial date will be set and the court will want to know the general nature of the defence, the witnesses required to give evidence, and any expert evidence that will be called at the trial. The court will also ask for notice of any legal arguments. All of these factors have some bearing on the length of the trial.

5.12 If the defendant is being prosecuted for an offence that involves compulsory or optional disqualification, and they hold a valid licence, then, whether it is posted to the court or brought on the day, the licence must be produced in time for the hearing.

EVIDENCE

5.13 Evidence (and the rules governing that evidence) in road traffic cases generally mirror other criminal offences. Common issues relate to the following:

- The identity of the driver.

- The owner of a vehicle. The court will accept a document from a police officer certifying that a car was being driven by, used by, or belonged to, a person on a specific occasion. A copy of this certificate must be given to the defendant at least seven days before the hearing or trial. The defendant can request that the officer attends the trial.

- Forensic evidence as to the proportion of alcohol or drugs in the defendant's blood, breath or urine. Challenging sample evidence or back-calculations are best left to an expert. The MG/DD forms need to be studied closely; the court will use the lowest reading of alcohol or drugs present in the defendant's system when the specimen was taken. See Chapter 10, and consider the 'hip-flask' defence if the defendant can show that they consumed alcohol/drugs before police took any sample but after the alleged offence.

THE TRIAL

5.14 There may be administrative hearings before the trial date. These hearings vary in scope and occur on a case-by-case basis, but they are intended to ensure that the trial runs as smoothly as possible. On the day of trial, the hearing begins with an opening by the prosecution. This is followed by the prosecution evidence, including any scientific material – for example, a statement confirming the accuracy of a road traffic camera, or forensic analysis. A defence expert may be needed to rebut prosecution evidence.

5.15   Once the prosecution evidence is concluded, the defendant might want to apply for the trial to be stopped. Most road traffic cases require the prosecution to meet the criminal standard of proof and therefore only succeed if the magistrates' bench or Crown Court jury are sure of the defendant's guilt. If there is no evidence to prove an essential element of the offence, or if the prosecution evidence has been so discredited or is so unreliable that no jury or court could safely convict, a defendant can make a submission that there is 'no case to answer' at the close of the prosecution case. This is sometimes referred to as a 'half time submission'. If the submission succeeds, a 'not guilty' verdict is entered. If you find yourself in this position, try to summarise your thoughts in writing. Regardless of the outcome, the defendant will be told the reasons for the decision by the court.

5.16   If the half time submission fails, then it falls to the defendant to present their case by calling evidence if they choose to do so. A defendant is not required to give evidence, but an adverse inference can be drawn by the court if they choose not to. Defence witnesses, including character witnesses, may also be called. Each party is then allowed to make closing speeches, in which they comment on the evidence which has been adduced during the trial. After hearing speeches, the magistrates or jury retire to decide the verdict.

TRIAL IN ABSENCE

5.17   Adjournments are often applied for in circumstances where the defendant fails to attend. If the defendant does not attend when they should, the general rule is that the court must proceed *as if* the defendant *were* present unless it is not in the interests of justice to do so – ie if it is unfair to continue. This rule does not apply where a defendant is under 18.

5.18   As mentioned above, a defendant can plead guilty in writing (ie by post) for summary offences. This is commonly referred to as a Section 12 Procedure (Magistrates' Courts Act 1980, s 12). Before the court can proceed under section 12, the defendant should have been sent a summons, an explanatory form, and a statement of the facts of the offence.

ADJOURNMENTS

5.19   If the case is adjourned in the absence of the defendant then, as long as all documents have been correctly served, the court has no obligation to inform the defendant of the next hearing date, provided the postponement is not more than four weeks (Magistrates' Courts Act 1980, s 12A(11)).

5.20   Where the defendant pleads guilty by post, but appears in court on the day of the hearing, they can, somewhat curiously, consent for the court to proceed as if they were absent. The court will allow the defendant to make representations in mitigation before sentence.

5.21   As a rule, the court should not accept an equivocal plea. A guilty plea must be absolute. For example, if the defendant is charged with driving at speed, the court cannot accept a plea in which they state that they are guilty but then claim not to have been the driver on that occasion.

SENTENCING

5.22   The defendant will need to be sentenced if they are convicted following a trial or a guilty plea. Generally, the process is the same in the magistrates' courts and Crown Court, with the important difference that the Crown Court has greater sentencing powers.

5.23   The prosecution outlines the facts of the offence (unless the defendant is being sentenced immediately after the trial or by the same judge who heard the case). The prosecutor will then refer to the sentencing guidelines concerning the offence. The guidelines are publicly available on the Sentencing Council's website.

5.24   The defendant will then have an opportunity to mitigate the sentence and for the court to explore aspects of the defendant's circumstances. This is a vital part of the process and should be prepared with as much information as possible. Written documents are the gold standard, so a letter from an employer, medical records, and a letter of support from friends or family will assist in persuading the court to impose a more lenient sentence.

APPEAL

5.25   Defendants can appeal against their conviction, sentence, or both, and the route of appeal and procedure vary depending upon which court dealt with the case.

5.26   For defendants tried in the magistrates' court, the procedure is relatively straightforward. The appeal is made to the Crown Court (as per sections 108 to 110 of the Magistrates' Courts Act 1980 and Part 34 of the Criminal Procedure Rules), and leave is not required unless the notice of appeal is served outside the 21-day time limit, which begins from the day of conviction or sentence, depending upon which is being appealed.

5.27   The appeal hearing in the Crown Court is heard by a judge (either a Circuit Judge or Crown Court Recorder) and two magistrates who did not preside over the original trial or sentencing hearing. The appeal is a complete rehearing. Therefore, if the appeal is against conviction, the trial will be repeated, with the same disputed witnesses giving evidence. The Crown Court cannot hear an appeal against conviction where a defendant has pleaded guilty in the magistrates' court.

5.28   Before appealing against a sentence imposed by the magistrates' court, consideration should first be given to whether an application can be made under section 142 of the Magistrates' Courts Act 1980. This provision enables the magistrates' court to rectify a mistake where the sentence or order made by that court is plainly wrong in law or has been imposed in error. If this does not apply, the appeal is made to the Crown Court in the same way as an appeal against conviction. As leave is not required, it is not unusual for defendants in road traffic cases to appeal to the Crown Court.

5.29   However, there are potential implications to be aware of. First, if the appeal is unsuccessful, the defendant will almost certainly be ordered to pay prosecution costs. These are typically around £600, but can be a lot more[1].

5.30   Second, the Crown Court has the power to increase, as well as reduce, the sentence imposed by the magistrates' court (albeit they are bound by the magistrates' sentencing powers). Clients should therefore be warned that an appeal carries the risk of making their situation worse.

5.31   There can be no appeal against an order of costs in the magistrates' court.

5.32   There are also circumstances in which an appeal can be made to the High Court. Either the prosecution or defence can appeal a decision of the magistrates' court on the basis that it is wrong in law or in excess of their jurisdiction (see Magistrates' Courts Act 1980, s 111). In short, where the issue is one of law, it can be considered by the High Court. Where, however, the issue concerns the finding made by the lower court on the facts, the appeal has to be made to the Crown Court. The same 21-day time limit for serving notice applies to appeals made to the High Court, and this cannot be extended by the magistrates' court.

5.33   Where a defendant is convicted or sentenced in the Crown Court, the appeal is made to the Court of Appeal (Criminal Appeal Act 1968, s 1). The time limit for submitting written grounds of appeal is 28 days from the date of the decision being appealed. Therefore, an appeal against conviction might

---

1   www.cps.gov.uk/legal-guidance/costs-annex-1.

have to be lodged before the defendant is sentenced, if the sentencing hearing is adjourned for more than 28 days. Unlike an appeal to the Crown Court, leave is required to appeal to the Court of Appeal. A conviction will not be quashed unless it is unsafe. This requires the Crown Court judge to have made an error of law, or for there to have been a serious irregularity during the trial, or, in limited circumstances, where there is important fresh evidence which was unavailable during the trial and which casts doubt on the jury's verdict. Where the sentence is appealed, leave will only be granted when it is arguable that the sentence imposed was manifestly excessive, or where it was wrong in law or principle.

Chapter 6

Journey of cases through the courts

Jack Barry

PRACTICAL ADVICE FOR THE ADVOCATE

6.1　　Road traffic cases typically begin with a 'postal requisition'. As the name suggests, this is a document, sent by post, which contains the charge and sets out the particulars of the alleged offence. A postal requisition will also contain details of the magistrates' court, and the date and time for the person charged (the defendant) to attend their first hearing.

6.2　　At the first hearing, often known as a 'plea hearing' or FTU ('first time up'), the court will want the defendant to either enter (or, in either-way offences, indicate) a plea of guilty or not guilty. This is despite the Initial Details of the Prosecution Case (IDPC) frequently only being supplied to the defending advocate on the day of the first hearing.

6.3　　Funding will also need to be put in place for the advocate to be paid for their attendance at the hearing. This can be by way of Legal Aid, but only if the defendant is eligible (this is far from automatic in road traffic cases).

6.4　　The IDPC is just that – the crux, or beginnings, of a case. It should contain a list of the charge(s), a case summary, and any key witness statements and key exhibits available at this stage of proceedings. The Crown should serve sufficient evidence to inform a plea of guilty or not guilty. Depending upon the strength of the evidence served, and the instructions of your lay client, advice will need to be given as to how the defendant should plead.

6.5　　When giving this initial advice, there are two key points which should always be canvassed with the client. The first is that a guilty plea at this stage will garner maximum credit from the court. This amounts to a one-third deduction from the sentence which would be imposed following a conviction after trial. Following the first hearing, the amount of available credit diminishes, and typically only 10% credit is afforded to those who plead guilty on the day of trial.

6.6   The second point relates to the allocation of the case. Whilst all offences start life in the magistrates' court, they are not all dealt with by this court and some are sent to the Crown Court. The magistrates' sentencing powers are such that some offences are simply too serious. These offences, such as causing death by dangerous driving, are indictable only, meaning that they can only be tried on indictment in the Crown Court. However, there are several offences which can be dealt with in either court. These are known as 'either-way' offences. The magistrates' decision as to whether an either-way case should be sent to the Crown Court, or retained by the magistrates' court, will depend upon the particular facts and complexity of the case. A key consideration will be the court's sentencing powers. The magistrates' court can impose a maximum sentence of 12 months' imprisonment for a single either-way offence (Judicial Review and Courts Act 2022, s 13), so more serious either-way offences are likely to be sent to the Crown Court.

6.7   When the defendant is arraigned and enters a plea to an either-way offence at the first hearing in the magistrates' court, the prosecution and defence advocates are invited to make representations as to where the matter should be heard, either as a trial (if the defendant pleads not guilty) or as a sentence hearing (if they plead guilty).

6.8   However, the defendant also has the right to elect a trial by jury in the Crown Court if they are charged with an either-way offence, regardless of whether the magistrates' court wishes to retain the case or not. This is something the advocate will need to advise their client on at the first hearing. If the defendant chooses not to elect Crown Court trial, and the magistrates accept that they have jurisdiction to either hear the trial or to sentence the defendant, the matter will remain in the magistrates' court. If the defendant pleads guilty to an either-way offence in the magistrates' court, they cannot elect to be sentenced by the Crown Court. It is for the magistrates to determine the venue for sentence.

6.9   If the magistrates decide that they do not have sufficient sentencing powers to proceed with the case in their court, or the defendant has elected a trial in the Crown Court, the matter will either:

(a)   be committed to the Crown Court for sentence – in the event of a guilty plea; or

(b)   be sent to the Crown Court for trial – in the event of a not guilty plea.

6.10   Some offences can only be dealt with in the magistrates' court. These are known as 'summary only' matters, and most road traffic offences fall within this category. These offences carry a maximum of six months' imprisonment. In the event that a guilty plea is entered at the first hearing, the magistrates can proceed to sentence straight away and often do so. Nevertheless, in situations where there exists important background information concerning the offence, or where the defendant is of previous good character or a youth (ie under 18 at the time of sentence), a pre-sentence report (PSR) can be prepared by the Probation Service. This often results in the sentence hearing being adjourned for a few weeks so that a written report can be prepared.

6.11   A PSR is available for all types of offence, and in both the magistrates' court and Crown Court. It will highlight the defendant's personal circumstances and factors influencing their offending behaviour, and will propose suitable non-custodial sentences where available. Of course, the court is not obliged to follow such a recommendation.

6.12   A defendant should only plead guilty if they *are* guilty of the offence, and it must be impressed upon them that the choice of whether to plead guilty lies with them – though this decision may be influenced by credit for an early guilty plea. Deciding whether to elect a trial in the Crown Court or choosing for it to remain in the magistrates' court is not always straightforward. Each carries its own advantages and disadvantages. One important consideration is cost. In the event that a defendant is convicted following a trial in the Crown Court, their costs towards the prosecution case will likely be a lot higher than they would have been in the magistrates' court.

6.13   Those paying privately will expect to pay more in professional fees for a trial in the Crown Court than in the magistrates' court. Full rights of audience are required in the Crown Court (meaning that the advocate can appear before any court in England and Wales) and, as a result, barristers are often instructed.

6.14   Magistrates' court trials will be conducted either by three lay members of the Bench, who decide upon the facts and take advice from their legal clerk, or one District Judge, who is legally qualified and therefore makes decisions about both facts and law. The reputation of District Judges is that they are generally more decisive and expeditious than three magistrates.

6.15   Crown Court trials are conducted in front of a jury who make decisions about the facts. The Circuit Judge or Recorder advises the jury as to the law. At the time of writing, there is a huge backlog in Crown Court trials. Delay is a feature which defendants will want to consider when deciding whether to elect or not; there is a long-held belief that juries are more easily swayed and have a lower conviction rate than magistrates, but a Crown Court trial is unlikely to happen within six months and could, in some parts of the country, be over a year away.

6.16   When a matter is sent for trial in the Crown Court, the first hearing to take place is known as a Plea and Trial Preparation Hearing (PTPH), which typically takes place a month after the first hearing in the magistrates' court.

6.17   The PTPH provides an opportunity for the defendant to have a conference with their advocate and for the evidence against them to be re-evaluated. Only 25 per cent credit is on offer for a guilty plea at this stage. In the event that the defendant maintains his not guilty plea, several stage dates are set by the court for the Crown and defence, and the trial date is set.

6.18   The stage dates are as follows:

- Stage one, which is typically 70 days from the date on which the case was sent to the Crown Court, or 50 days if the defendant is in custody. The prosecution must serve the bulk of their evidence by this date and any 'unused material' (unused evidence), which is capable of assisting the defence case, or undermining the prosecution case.

- Stage two is to be completed 28 days after stage one. The defence must serve their defence statement, setting out the client's case, and a list of witnesses they may require at trial. This witness list should include prosecution witnesses who the defence intend to cross-examine, and any defence witnesses.

- Stage three is the Crown's opportunity to respond to the defence statement by providing further material to the defence, either as served evidence or unused material (although the prosecution are required to maintain a continued review of disclosure throughout the proceedings). Stage three is generally completed within a month of stage two.

- Sometimes, a stage four date is set, as a marked last opportunity for the defence to provide material, or make any applications, arising out of prosecution disclosure.

6.19   Stage dates are not aspirational; they must be closely followed by both the Crown and defence. Applications to extend such dates without good reason rarely succeed, although the court will be mindful of achieving the overriding objective of a fair trial. In the magistrates' court, once a guilty plea has been entered or the client has been convicted after trial, there may be alternative disposals which are available as part of the sentencing regime, or as an effective part of mitigation.

DRIVING COURSES

6.20   Eligibility for attendance on a National Driver Offender Retraining Scheme (NDORS) course can be either an out-of-court disposal, or a way of mitigating the sentence for a defendant. The driver must hold a valid driving licence at the time of the offence and be prepared to pay the course fee. The schemes are operated on behalf of the police and can, in certain circumstances, be offered to a driver as an alternative to prosecution.

6.21   For example, the National Driver Alertness course is one such course that is usually only available to drivers involved in a collision where there is enough evidence to warrant a prosecution for careless driving under the Road Traffic Act 1988 (RTA 1988, s 3). The decision as to eligibility for this course is case-specific, and will ultimately depend upon the driving involved. This is one means of alternative or out-of-court disposal, but this is only appropriate in more minor cases.

6.22   There are clear factors which must be applied by the police, Crown Prosecution Service and courts when considering the imposition of a NDORS course:

(a)   There must be a realistic prospect of conviction for the alleged offence. It is not possible to offer a NDORS course for one offence and then prosecute or issue fixed penalty points for other offences arising from the same incident. Sometimes, no further action is taken in relation to other minor offences that occurred at the time.

(b)   A course cannot be offered within three years of any previous offence that has been dealt with by a similar NDORS course.

6.23   In cases which have already proceeded to sentence in the magistrates' court, the magistrates can offer the defendant a place on a Drink Drive Rehabilitation course which can be imposed upon defendants who are found guilty of a drink drive offence and whose driving ban is to run for a period of 12 months or more. These courses, carried out by approved providers, can reduce the period over which somebody is disqualified from driving by up to a quarter, provided the course is completed within a specified time period. The defendant will need to pay for this course themselves and it can cost up to £250. Crucially, however, a decision must be made on the day in court; a defendant cannot change their mind later if they have initially declined to undertake the course.

Part 3

Offences

Chapter 7

Speeding

Susan Cavender

7.1   Speed limits are a source of great revenue for the government, and frequently – if caught breaching those limits – a source of great misery and annoyance for the general motorist. From the time of their introduction, speed limits have been under constant review. The first speed limit, introduced in 1934 because of high casualty rates, was 30mph in built-up areas. Several decades later, in 1967, the 70mph limit on motorways was brought in for similar reasons. Aside from a temporary reduction in 1973 during the oil crisis, this has remained the maximum speed on motorways and most dual carriageways. Since 1977, the default speed on most other unrestricted roads is 60mph.

7.2   Recent press reports suggest that revision is underway again. Casualties on country roads now account for 57% of fatalities, despite only carrying 43% of the traffic, and, at the time of writing (August 2022), Surrey County Council is intending to trial speed limits of 20–30mph across 80 square miles on rural roads between Guildford and Dorking.

7.3   Given that, in urban areas, a reduction in speed to 20mph has been shown to increase numbers of both cyclists and pedestrians (a 20mph limit is now common in many towns and cities), it is likely that reduced speed limits on country roads will become commonplace; annoying for drivers but providing a welcome relief to cyclists and pedestrians. The rules about maximum speeds differ depending on the type of road and the type of vehicle. The default speed limit, known as the 'national speed limit', varies depending upon these factors.

7.4   Most vans and all heavy goods vehicles have a lower speed limit than cars, and motorhomes can have different speed limits depending on their weight. Different limits apply to vehicles which tow trailers, are articulated, and/or are agricultural vehicles. The limits for different classes of vehicles are set out in section 86 of, and Schedule 6 to, the Road Traffic Regulation Act 1984 ('RTRA 1984'). If in doubt, these are clarified on the government website[1].

---

1   www.gov.uk/speed-limits.

7.5   We are probably all familiar with the general rules set out in the RTRA 1984:

- All 'restricted' roads carry a 30mph speed limit (see below for definition).

- Many urban centres are now set at 20mph; a decision which can be made by the local authority.

- The 'national' speed limit on most other roads is 60mph.

- Dual carriageways, with a permanent barrier between carriageways, carry a 70mph limit.

- The motorway speed limit is 70mph.

- Temporary speed limits can be set for up to 18 months and for a variety of periods or times (see RTRA 1984, s 88 and, for roadworks, RTRA 1984, s 14).

- Some speed limits apply to specific locations (for example, in Royal Parks or the Port of London).

7.6   A restricted road is defined as any road with streetlights every 200 yards or less (RTRA 1984, ss 81 and 82). The mere fact that the *signs* are not visible is not a defence; if 'a system of street lighting' can be seen, you are in a 30mph limit[2]. Broken streetlights are no defence; if the 'system' of streetlighting is in place with lights at regular intervals, a 30mph limit applies. There are no excuses! If there is a system of streetlights in place, but the limit is higher than 30mph, this will be clear from signs attached to lampposts.

7.7   Traffic signs must indicate the speed for any particular stretch of road; if there are streetlights but no signs, it is *always* a 30mph zone. The beginning of a regulated speed zone must be indicated by signs, with repeat signs at regular intervals. Where a temporary speed limit is inadequately signed, this failure to comply with the requirements can be sufficient to quash any fines arising from breaches of the temporary speed limit.

7.8   The size, colour and reflectivity requirements for regulatory signs are set out in Schedule 10 to the Traffic Signs Regulations and General Directions 2016[3]. Signs indicating the beginning or end of a speed limit on a trunk or main road should be illuminated, or within 50 metres of a streetlamp, to make them visible.

---

2   *Hood v Lewis* [1976] RTR 99.
3   SI 2016/362.

7.9   Although emergency services vehicles (fire engines, ambulances, police cars etc) must abide by speed limits in general, an exemption applies if keeping within the speed limit would 'hinder the use of the vehicle for the purpose for which it is being used on that occasion' (RTRA 1984, s 87). For police, this exemption only includes officers who have been trained to drive at high speeds, but it does allow for officers to be trained by another experienced officer. However, the very broadly drafted phrase 'purpose for which it is being used on that occasion' presumably does not allow police officers to blue-light it back to the station for tea!

7.10   What counts as circumstances which are within the exemption is always considered in the specific context of each case[4]. Further exemptions are likely to come into force if and when section 19 of the Road Safety Act 2006 replaces section 87 of the RTRA 1984.

7.11   A defence of necessity can apply and can include an unexpected event such as natural disaster or sudden illness to the driver or a passenger. This is narrowly interpreted; it would not cover an emergency such as taking a child to hospital with a broken leg which, in itself, is not life-threatening[5].

7.12   Evidence of excess speed is usually provided by:

- Vascar (Visual Average Speed Computer and Recorder) which is an average speed check over a stretch of road. This, more than any other device, has forced drivers to comply with temporary areas of reduced speed, especially on motorways. The longest single enforceable section is on the A9 which runs through the Highlands of Scotland.

- Speed cameras from mobile units. Each police force publishes a schedule showing the daily positioning of mobile cameras.

- Hand-held cameras used by neighbourhood residents who have been trained in their use.

- Radar speed meters/radar guns. Radar is less reliable than cameras: it is important to ensure that the certification is up-to-date and that the officer is suitably qualified to use one. These devices can give false readings (as a result of low batteries, or the beam bouncing off something other than the target car).

- Hand-held laser speed device.

- Dash-cams from police cars.

4   *DPP v Milton* [2006] EWHC 242 (Admin).
5   *Pipe v DPP* [2012] EWHC 1821 (Admin).

- Witness testimony (often police officers), although this must be from more than one witness, and both witnesses must have seen the speeding at the same moment. Officers who witness speeding by the same car on different stretches of road will not suffice. These caveats are codified in section 89(2) of the RTRA 1984; and see also the case of *Brighty v Pearson*[6]. An officer's testimony as to the speed of a vehicle, which is supported by a reading from his speedometer, or a radar gun, is sufficient even where the speedometer has not been tested for accuracy[7].

7.13   Speed checking equipment is, of course, evidence and is generally conclusive. Section 20 of the Road Traffic Offenders Act 1988 ('RTOA 1988') sets out the rules governing the admissibility of evidence from 'prescribed devices', which include any such device specified by the Secretary of State by statutory instrument. As you would expect, a large number of such devices have been approved, and the list can be easily expanded.

7.14   Proof that a device is functioning correctly can be adduced in evidence. In most cases, a certificate to this effect is served at least seven days before trial. A defendant can also request that the witness who signed the certificate attend the trial. There are cases in which the evidence produced from the different types of devices has been tested, but this has become less common and, on the whole, the general presumption is that they are working properly.

7.15   A Notice of Intended Prosecution (NIP) must be sent prior to prosecution for speeding offences, whether for permanent or temporary speed restrictions, on all roads including motorways (RTOA 1988, s 1). The old habit of warning other drivers that they are about to approach a speed check was found not to be obstructive, on the grounds that the driver was preventing other drivers from committing an offence[8]; this interpretation has, nevertheless, since been criticised by the Divisional Court. By contrast, using a laser-jammer to prevent the police from taking an accurate reading of speed has resulted in a conviction and immediate imprisonment[9].

7.16   The following table sets out the penalties for offences under the RTRA 1984. All of the offences listed are summary only. Disqualification is discretionary for all bar the minimum speed limit offence, for which it does not apply:

---

6   [1938] 4 All ER 127.
7   *Nicholas v Penny* [1950] 2 All ER 89; *Swain v Gillett* [1974] RTR 446.
8   *Bastable v Little* [1907] 1 KB 59.
9   *R v Burke* [2019] EWCA Crim 928.

Offence	RTRA 1984 Section	Fine	Penalty Points	Endorsement Code
Exceeding general speed limit for road	s 89	Level 3	3–6	SP30
Exceeding speed limit for goods vehicles	s 89	Level 3	3–6	SP10
Exceeding speed limit for type of vehicle	s 89	Level 3	3–6	SP20
Exceeding speed limit for passenger vehicles	s 89	Level 3	3–6	SP40
Exceeding overall speed limit for motorway	s 17(4)	Level 4	3–6	SP50
Exceeding lower speed limit for vehicle on motorway	s 89	Level 3	3–6	SP10, SP20 or SP40, as appropriate
Temporary speed restriction for roadworks etc	s 16(1)	Level 3	3–6	SP60
Minimum speed limit	s 88(7)	Level 3	–	–

MAXIMUM POINTS

7.17   Someone with an accumulation of 12 points or more is known as a 'totter'; this number of points results in immediate disqualification for a minimum of six months, (RTOA 1988, s 35) unless 'exceptional hardship' is proven (see Chapter 20).

7.18   This is an iron rule; speed cameras can result in a driver being caught (if they are very unlucky) several times in quick succession. Even if the speed recorded in each offence is relatively low, each infraction results in another three points which remain on the licence for three years. It is easy to see how these can multiply until a driver risks losing their licence for six months as a result of what they consider to be more bad luck than bad driving.

7.19   Once the maximum of 12 points is reached, the Sentencing Council guideline on 'totting up' disqualification states that the minimum period for disqualification is as follows:

●   **six months** if no previous disqualification is to be taken into account;

●   **one year** if one previous disqualification is to be taken into account; and

- **two years** if more than one previous disqualification is to be taken into account.

7.20   A previous disqualification is to be taken into account if it is:

- not less than **56 days**; and

- **imposed** within the three years immediately preceding the **date on which the current offence** (or most recent of the current offences) **was committed**.

7.21   There is one small compensation: unlike other disqualifications, totting up disqualifications erase all penalty points.

SPEED AWARENESS COURSES

7.22   For those who are detected driving slightly above the relevant speed limit, there is (often) the option to do a speed awareness course and, by doing so, avoid three penalty points.

7.23   The courses can be done more than once (I have to admit to having completed three courses in the past 20 years!) but will not be offered if the driver has a similar speeding offence within the last three years.

7.24   The criteria are tight, and vary between different police areas, but in general the detected speed must be no more than 10% or 10mph above the limit, so it is common to find people who were caught doing 38mph in a 30mph limit. The course, if available, costs the same as the fine, and takes up about three hours of time, but it is well worth it because it avoids three penalty points, and penalty points mean prizes – in the shape of increased insurance premiums which no-one wants.

7.25   The offer of a course is made after the NIP has been returned confirming that the registered keeper was the driver; if that was not the case, a fresh NIP is sent to the driver at the time of the speeding; presuming that they accept the speeding, they may then be offered a course.

7.26   The courses are sometimes run by the local police force, sometimes by private companies and, since the pandemic, are often conducted online. They are informative and thought-provoking, intended to ensure that drivers leave with a better understanding of the law and in the hope that they will be better drivers in the future.

Chapter 8

Acquisitive offences

Grace Flynn

8.1   Cars and other vehicles are a tempting prospect for thieves. We probably all know someone who has been the victim of a car-related theft, if we have not been such a victim ourselves. The motivation for stealing a vehicle does, however, vary (not that it is of any comfort to the owner!).

8.2   Some are never to be seen again, others simply used and dumped once the purpose for which they were taken is over. A shiny new Range Rover or a top-of-the-range motorbike are attractive targets for those wanting to make a swift profit through an 'acquisitive' offence. Then there are vehicles used for a quick spin or stolen to order as a getaway vehicle for use in another crime.

This chapter will outline the main acquisitive offences.

8.3   The key factor underlying these offences is the intention of the defendant. What was in their mind at the time of committing the offence and can this be proven?

8.4   An awareness of the 'mens rea' test for each offence can be the difference between a summary only or more serious charge.

OFFENCES

8.5

- Theft of a vehicle (Theft Act 1968, s 7).

- Taking motor vehicle or other conveyance without authority (Theft Act 1968, s 12).

- Aggravated Vehicle Taking (Aggravated TWOC) (Theft Act 1968, s 12A).

- Interfering with a vehicle (Criminal Attempts Act 1981, s 9).

THEFT OF A VEHICLE, OR TAKING A VEHICLE WITHOUT CONSENT? THE DIFFERENCE

8.6   The theft of a vehicle comes under the standard definition of theft: *dishonestly taking* a vehicle *belonging to another* with the *intention of permanently depriving* the owner of it.

8.7   Intention is key. It is the intention to permanently deprive that distinguishes theft from the offence of taking a vehicle without consent ('TWOC').

8.8   With TWOC, also known as 'joyriding', the vehicle is taken temporarily and abandoned, for example, at the roadside.

8.9   Theft generally involves an intention to sell the vehicle, sometimes split up for parts, with the aim that it does not make its way back to the owner, and for the taker to make a financial benefit from the offence.

8.10   In TWOC, the intention is in a sense a more careless one; taking the vehicle and leaving it, perhaps to be returned to the owner if the police happen to find it or if a member of the public comes across it and reports it.

8.11   The defence, as outlined below, is for the taker to establish that he believed that he had the owner's consent to take the vehicle.

8.12   In respect of the offence of TWOC, it is also an offence to be 'carried' (as a passenger) in a vehicle that has been taken without the owner's consent. The prosecution must prove that the passenger was aware that the vehicle had been unlawfully taken in the first place.

8.13   It is a defence to show that the passenger believed that the driver was permitted to have the vehicle during the time period in which they were being carried. In an ideal world, text messages from the driver offering the passenger a lift in their new car that they have just purchased (!) might help point to the ignorance and innocence of the passenger. However, if the driver has a significant criminal record for TWOC which the passenger was fully aware of, that will make establishing the defence of ignorance somewhat harder. All will revolve around circumstantial evidence.

8.14   Of course, the victim ('loser') will not know whether or not their vehicle has been taken on a temporary basis when they first notice that it is missing; all they know is that their property has been taken and they want it returned.

8.15   A decision as to which offence should be prosecuted will generally depend upon an assessment of the overall circumstances in which the vehicle was eventually recovered (if it was recovered). This may assist in establishing the original intention. For example, a car which is quickly sold on to another was obviously taken as a theft, whereas a car left abandoned on the roadside was most likely taken without consent.

8.16   Although the differences in law between the offences may be subtle, there is a significant disparity in sentence. TWOC is a summary-only offence with a maximum sentence of a level 5 fine and/or six months' imprisonment. Aggravated TWOC is an either-way offence with a maximum sentence of two years' custody. Theft, however, is either way, with a maximum sentence of seven years.

8.17   Whilst the maximum sentence is, of course, unlikely, penalties can be harsh for repeat offenders and, if the offence is added to dangerous driving or causing death/serious injury in the stolen vehicle, the impact on sentence could be severe.

8.18   It is also relevant to consider how driving a stolen or 'TWOC'd' vehicle will inevitably have an impact on other aspects of driving law mentioned in this book. For example, there will be no valid insurance policy to cover the driving of the stolen vehicle. This is an aggravating feature that will need to be considered and mitigated.

THEFT OF A VEHICLE (THEFT ACT 1968, s 7)

8.19   A defendant is guilty of theft if they:

(i)   dishonestly

(ii)   appropriate a vehicle

(iii)   belonging to another

(iv)   with the intention of permanently depriving the other of it.

8.20   A defence to theft will depend upon eliminating one of the above elements, so each will need to be carefully considered. Was the behaviour dishonest? Did the vehicle actually belong to someone else? Had it been 'borrowed' from a close family member? What was the defendant's intention in taking it? Was it 'dishonest'?

TAKING A MOTOR VEHICLE OR OTHER CONVEYANCE WITHOUT AUTHORITY (THEFT ACT 1968, s 12)

8.21   A defendant is guilty if:

(i)   without having the consent of the owner or other lawful authority,

(ii)   they take any conveyance for their own or another's use,

OR

(iii)   knowing that any conveyance has been taken without such authority,

(iv)   they drive it or allow themselves to be carried in or on it.

8.22   TWOC is available as an alternative offence in a trial in the Crown Court for theft of a vehicle. The jury may, therefore, convict the defendant of the lesser offence, meaning that the maximum sentence is capped at that available for a summary-only matter[1]. If charged with theft, a defendant might offer a guilty plea to TWOC as a less serious alternative to a theft charge. It should be noted that an offence under section 12(5) (taking a bicycle) is summary only and can only be punished with a fine (maximum level 3.)

DEFENCE TO TWOC (THEFT ACT 1968, s 12(6))

8.23   It is a defence for the defendant to prove that they believed that they had, or would have had, the owner's consent to use the vehicle, if the owner had known the circumstances in which they took it:

> 'A person does not commit an offence under this section by anything done in the belief that he has lawful authority to do it or that he would have the owner's consent if the owner knew of his doing it and the circumstances of it.'

8.24   The defence to TWOC is for the defendant to establish that they genuinely believed that they had the owner's permission. Again, this will hinge on an assessment of the circumstances and be for the defendant to establish why it was that they held that belief.

AGGRAVATED VEHICLE TAKING (AGGRAVATED TWOC) (THEFT ACT 1968, s 12A)

8.25   A defendant is guilty of aggravated TWOC if he commits the basic offence and, whilst the vehicle was being driven (before it was recovered), one or more of the following occurred:

(i)   the vehicle was driven dangerously on a road or other public place;

---

1   Theft Act 1968, s 12(4).

(ii)   owing to the driving of the vehicle, injury was caused to a person;

(iii) owing to the driving of the vehicle, damage was caused to any property, other than the vehicle; and

(iv)   damage was caused to the vehicle.

8.26   The definition of 'dangerous driving' for the purposes of this section is identical to that of section 2 of the Road Traffic Act 1988 ('RTA 1988').

8.27   The classic example of aggravated TWOC would be the taking of a car for a joy-ride, it being driven far below the standard expected of a careful and competent driver (usually speeding, overtaking dangerously etc), before crashing into other parked cars or a wall and coming to a halt.

8.28   'Recovery' is defined as when a vehicle 'is restored to its owner or to other lawful possession or custody' – in short, when the vehicle has been seized and impounded by the police or collected from the scene by the owner.

8.29   It is a defence if the defendant can prove that either:

(i)   the driving, accident or damage occurred *before* he committed the basic offence of TWOC; or

(ii)   he was *neither in, nor on, nor in the immediate vicinity of* the vehicle when that driving, accident or damage occurred.

8.30   The maximum sentence for aggravated TWOC is, on indictment, two years' imprisonment. If the accident caused by the dangerous driving led to the death of the injured person, the maximum is 14 years.

8.31   The basic TWOC offence is available as an alternative for a jury that acquits of the aggravated version. In that situation, the Crown Court is to sentence as if it were dealing with TWOC in the magistrates' court.

INTERFERING WITH A VEHICLE (CRIMINAL ATTEMPTS ACT 1981, s 9)

8.32   The offence of vehicle interference is perhaps best thought of as analogous to an attempted theft or attempt to take a vehicle without consent, which is why it is codified under the Criminal Attempts Act 1981.

8.33   As with the other offences, the elements that the prosecution must prove concern the intention of the defendant.

8.34   It must be proved that the defendant interfered with the vehicle (or trailer[2]) with the intention of:

(a)   going on to steal the vehicle;

(b)   stealing something from the vehicle; or

(c)   taking it without consent.

It could also be that the defendant interfered with the vehicle in order to enable someone else to commit one of the above three offences.

8.35   This is a summary only offence, with a maximum sentence of three months' imprisonment and/or a level 4 fine.

8.36   There is no definition of 'interference', which will be a matter of fact to be argued on a case-by-case basis. There has to be an act involving some degree of interference in addition to the relevant intention. Active steps must be taken. For example, simply peering through a window to assess the prospects of stealing would not be classed as interference, because nothing has actually been done. However, actively trying to force open a car door could be classed as sufficient effort to amount to interference. More obvious would be smashing a window or sliding a tool down the side to open it. Interestingly, the simple act of placing a hand on a door handle, and the question as to whether that can be classed as 'interference', remains ambiguous[3].

8.37   In short, interference should be given its natural meaning and, as a general guide, should include some positive act. If in doubt, it seems it should be considered on a common sense basis in each case.

8.38   Interference is treated most severely by the courts where there is an element of professionalism or organisation about the activity – for example, a clear leadership role and this being shown to be part of an enterprise to steal cars to order. Damage caused to the vehicle is also highly relevant; were the vehicle to be left in a dangerous condition, with a risk that the owner might drive it unaware of the damage caused, the potential for harm is high.

8.39   Tampering with a vehicle (RTA 1988, s 25) involves getting onto a vehicle or tampering with the brakes or another part of the vehicle's mechanism and only applies to vehicles on a road or parked on a space 'provided by a local authority'. Section 26 of the RTA 1988 prohibits getting onto a vehicle or trailer which is in motion on a road. These offences are not endorsable but do carry fines.

---

2   'Motor vehicle' and 'trailer' are defined under Road Traffic Act 1988, s 185(1).
3   *Reynolds and Warren v Metropolitan Police* [1982] Crim LR 831.

Chapter 9

Regulatory offences

Susan Cavender

CONSTRUCTION OF VEHICLES AND THEIR USAGE

9.1 It is a relief to anyone who drives or is carried in a mechanised vehicle to know that there are a great number of regulations relating to both the construction and usage of motor vehicles. The Road Vehicles (Construction and Use) Regulations 1986 ('Construction and Use Regulations')[1] are the core piece of legislation, though now much amended.

9.2 Whilst the UK was in the EU these regulations were gradually being replaced by EU 'type approval' schemes. This is now changing and, since Brexit, an interim arrangement has been put in place until 31 December 2022 which enables the Secretary of State to issue 'type approval' certificates.

9.3 It is illegal to drive a vehicle on the roads unless the construction has been approved and a certificate obtained; for the purposes of this book, we do not intend to go into these regulations in any depth, but the details can be found in the Road Vehicles (Approval) Regulations 2020[2] (for those who build a one-off vehicle and need to get it approved, see reg 18).

9.4 There are separate regulations covering the manufacture of different types of vehicle, including motorcycles, tractors, and agricultural or forestry vehicles. Whilst the regulations relate to both motor vehicles and their component parts, they do not apply to trailers which are not vehicles in their own right.

9.5 It is an offence to sell a vehicle which does not have a certificate of conformity, or the Secretary of State's approval certificate (RTA 1988, s 65)

---

1   SI 1986/1078.
2   SI 2020/818.

and it is also an offence to sell a vehicle which is in an unroadworthy condition (RTA 1988, s 75).

9.6   Vehicles of every type must be well (ie safely) constructed. The Pedal Cycles (Construction and Use) Regulations 1983[3] includes both bicycles and e-bikes. There are specific speed restrictions for electric bikes; both e-scooters and e-bikes are classified and regulated as motor vehicles (see Chapter 2).

9.7   Be aware that some offences – principally those relating to causation of danger – may be covered by regulations relating to both construction *and* usage.

9.8   The detailed regulations cover the need, and standards of manufacture, for essential items such as speedometers (with some exceptions, Construction and Use Regulations, regs 35 and 36) and brakes, including every part of a braking system (Construction and Use Regulations, regs 15–18, Sch 3), and set out requirements for various types and sizes of vehicle.

9.9   Other provisions of the Construction and Use Regulations cover different aspects of the construction and use of vehicles:

- Regulation 33 – mirrors: different types and sized are required for different sized vehicles.

- Regulations 37 and 99 – horns, and anything which acts as a 'warning instrument'.

- Regulation 39 – fuel tanks.

- Regulation 53 – emblem or mascot on the bonnet.

- Regulation 54 – exhaust system and silencer (reg 57 for motorbikes).

- Regulation 55 – silencers.

- Regulation 61 – emissions; this will vary depending on the type and age of the vehicle.

- Regulation 63 – wings/mudguards (exemptions apply to some vehicles).

- Regulation 109 – televisions in cars which are visible from the driver's seat are banned.

- Regulation 110 – mobile phones; it is commonly known that hand-held mobiles/radios etc cannot be used at all by drivers, though there are limited exemptions in case of true emergency.

---

3   SI 1983/1176.

9.10   The way in which the regulations cover not only construction but also usage is apparent in regulation 107, which states that a vehicle must not be left unattended unless the brakes are on and the engine off, which seems so obvious as to hardly need stating.

9.11   Vehicles cannot be used on the road if the tyres are unsuitable, and the definition of a defective tyre is set out in section 41A of the RTA 1988 and regulation 27(1) of the Construction and Use Regulations which specifies 11 different types of defects which include general suitability, proper inflation, and the tread patterns of tyres ('tread pattern', 'original tread pattern' and 'breadth of tread' are all defined).

9.12   There are specific regulations and exceptions which apply to specific vehicles such as agricultural equipment (especially 'trailed appliances'), and detailed conditions covering maximum length, width, height (maximum of 4.67m for a bus) and overhang specifications.

9.13   In certain circumstances, the police must be given at least two days' notice if exceptional vehicles are to be used on the roads, and it is illegal for a trailer which exceeds 18.65m to be used on a road without the police being informed. The regulations extend to stipulating the rear markings on large vehicles over 7500kg.

9.14   If you need to know whether the vehicle you are concerned with is an 'agricultural trailed appliance' or a 'living van' or a 'works truck', and many definitions inbetween, detailed definitions can be found in the Construction and Use Regulations.

9.15   How a vehicle is classified can make a big difference, especially if prosecution is pending, and it is essential that the correct regulations are applied. The onus falls upon the defendant to establish any features which put a vehicle into a particular class, especially if it is not immediately apparent on inspection[4].

9.16   The test if such a breach of regulations comes to court is the lower civil test (balance of probabilities). The penalty upon conviction is a fine, which can be unlimited in certain circumstances, plus endorsement (any endorsable offence under the Construction and Use Regulations carries three penalty points), and – in serious cases – disqualification.

9.17   The different routes to prosecution – either under a regulation or under the RTA 1988 – and consequent range of sentence are best explained by the

---

4   *Wakeman v Catlow* [1977] RTR 174.

following example which demonstrates the need to check carefully the section used in the charge which will impact upon the eventual sentence.

9.18 If a breach of regulation100 of the Construction and Use Regulations (Maintenance and use so as not to be a danger) is alleged, the proceedings must be brought under section 42 of the RTA 1988 (Breach of other construction and use requirements), with the consequence that, on conviction, there are no powers of disqualification or endorsement.

9.19 If, on the other hand, a prosecution is brought under section 40A of the RTA 1988 (Using a vehicle in a dangerous condition), the consequences, on conviction, could be discretionary disqualification and obligatory endorsement as mentioned above.

9.20 Be aware that, if a second offence under section 40A of the RTA 1988 is committed within three years of the first, then disqualification is obligatory. The minimum period of disqualification will be six months: see Road Traffic Offenders Act 1988, s 34(4B).

LOADS

9.21 Unsurprisingly, there are regulations which prevent the use of either vehicles or their load which are liable to cause nuisance or are in a dangerous condition. Prosecutions can be brought under regulation 100(2) and (3) if both danger and nuisance may be caused.

9.22 Section 40A of the RTA 1988 (Using a vehicle in a dangerous condition) provides express statutory authority for dealing with the use of vehicles in a dangerous condition:

'A person is guilty of an offence if he uses, or causes or permits another to use, a motor vehicle or trailer on a road when–

(a) the condition of the motor vehicle or trailer, or of its accessories or equipment, or

(b) the purpose for which it is used, or

(c) the number of passengers carried by it, or the manner in which they are carried, or

(d) the weight, position or distribution of its load, or the manner in which it is secured,

is such that the use of the motor vehicle or trailer involves a danger of injury to any person.'

9.23   Section 41B(2) of the RTA 1988 sets out limited statutory defences, which include the vehicle being on its way to a weighbridge, or being less than 5% over its load limit. The burden of proof in such cases falls on the defendant. The test is objective; it is not whether or not the driver *believed* that his passenger was safe, but whether there was an *objective* danger of injury.

9.24   When a Mr Gray took his seven-year-old boy on a short journey through London sitting on the wheel arch in the back of an open Jeep, holding onto the roll bars and occasionally standing up, he was understandably convicted under section 40A(c) of the RTA 1988[5]. Whilst the manner of driving is relevant, the court is concerned with the mere possibility of injury being caused as a result of the ordinary risks of driving, such as sudden braking or swerving, stopping or turning.

9.25   Regulation 100 of the Construction and Use Regulations is designed to ensure that vehicles are not in a condition to cause danger or nuisance when driving on the roads. The three paragraphs (which are couched in terms of double negatives) need to be carefully considered if charges are brought, to ensure that the correct provision is used.

9.26   Regulation 100 can be summarised as follows:

(1)   A vehicle and trailer and all parts thereof must be in such condition as to cause no *danger* to anyone or to vehicles or other property; this is including the number of passengers, the way in which they are carried, and the weight, distribution and packing of any load carried on the vehicle.

(2)   Any load must be secured so that no *danger or nuisance* is *likely* to be caused by the load falling/being blown off the vehicle or by movement of the vehicle.

(3)   No vehicle can be used for any unsuitable purpose so as to cause a *danger or nuisance* to other road users.

9.27   Offences under regulation 100 would include, for example:

- a load falling from, or being knocked off, a lorry;

- trees trunks protruding well beyond the back of a trailer;

- a van driven with the tailboard down;

- a steering wheel with excessive play in the joint; and

- a tow bar which uncoupled because it was not correctly attached.

---

5   *Gray v DPP* [1999] RTR 339.

9.28   The case law demonstrates that a good degree of common sense is expected from the drivers and owners or operators of machinery and vehicles on the roads.

9.29   Under section 75 of the RTA 1988 (and regulations), it is illegal to offer to sell or supply a vehicle which is not in roadworthy condition, or which would cause the danger of injury to anyone if used on a road, unless the seller takes all steps to make sure that the potential buyer is aware of the true condition of the vehicle; this would include the alteration of a vehicle or trailer in such a way as to make it a potential danger to others. It may seem somewhat artificial but, because an auctioneer is simply requesting bids from potential buyers, rather than offering to sell vehicles, auction houses are not caught by this section.

LIGHTING

9.30   Lighting is covered by specific regulations, namely the Road Vehicles Lighting Regulations 1989, which cover all vehicles except bicycles, which are dealt with by section 81 of the RTA 1988.

9.31   The regulations, which apply to all vehicles used on a road, set out what is required in terms of lamps, the number and position of headlamps, retro-reflectors, rear markings, and lights for registration plates. The individual requirements for different types of vehicle are set out in seven tables of Schedule 1.

9.32   The colour of lights front and rear, fog lights, limitation on flashing lights, lighting for trailers or vehicles being towed, and overhanging loads are all covered, as are other details including the front and rear signage needed by school buses. All lights must be properly maintained and working and must be in use if there is 'serious reduced visibility' or – obviously – after sunset.

9.33   There are some limited exemptions which apply to some vehicles in daylight hours, expressed as 'between sunrise and sunset', and include horse-drawn vehicles (which can be drawn by any animal!), bicycles and invalid carriages.

TEST CERTIFICATES

9.34   Every vehicle more than three years old (ie first registered more than three years ago) and used on a road must pass the MOT (Ministry of Transport) test: (RTA 1988, s 47). The time limit is shortened to one year for minibuses and other vehicles with more than eight passenger seats. It is use on the road which triggers the need for a test, and such use without a test certificate is an offence.

9.35 Test certificates can only be provided by 'authorised examiners', who must set out the reasons for refusal. Exemptions (see Motor Vehicles (Tests) Regulations 1981, SI 1981/1694, reg 6) apply for a variety of different types of vehicle, such as locomotives, motor tractors, works trucks and pedestrian-controlled vehicles. There is an exemption under regulation 6(2)(a) to cover the vehicle being driven to a test centre where it has been booked in for a test, but the regulations are tightly worded and do not cover driving to a test centre without prior arrangement.

SEAT BELTS

9.36 Everyone knows that seat belts are compulsory and have been for some time. Since 1968, all road vehicles have needed to have seat belts installed, and their use has been a legal requirement for anyone travelling in a front seat since January 1983. In 1989, the law changed to require children under 14 carried in the back seats to be strapped in and, since 1991, this has also been the case for adults in back seats.

9.37 The justification is borne out by the figures which suggest that seatbelts are 50% effective in preventing fatal injuries for drivers, and greatly reduce serious injuries (45%) and minor injuries (25%), resulting in an estimated saving of thousands of lives since they were introduced[6].

9.38 There are exceptions, most obviously in vintage cars which do not have seat belts fitted, but also for a driver who is reversing, for any of the emergency services, for the driver of a goods vehicle driving no more than 50 metres between stops, and a licensed taxi driver. If a medical exemption is required, a doctor can be requested to provide an exemption certificate. Failure to wear a seatbelt can result in prosecution and a fine. There has been discussion in the press about points being imposed, but no legislation has yet been drafted.

9.39 Regulations under section 15A of the RTA 1988 set out the requirements for child seats. An offence is committed by anyone who sells or hires child seats which do not meet the requisite standard, although there is a defence available if the items were intended for sale for export.

PROTECTIVE HEADGEAR

9.40 Helmets are compulsory for any motorbike, with or without a side car, which is defined as such and for any moped. This strict law applies to anyone

---

6   Road Safety Observatory.

driving or riding as a passenger on a motorbike; they must wear a helmet and it must comply with British Standards specifications.

9.41   To wear a helmet without properly fastening it is an offence. There are a few exceptions – most famously for Sikh motorcyclists who have been exempt since 1976 – but also for some types of vehicle, such as mowing machinery, or for someone pushing a motor bike.

Chapter 10

Drink/drug driving

Mark Linehan

'... this legislation, contrary to the general traditions of the criminal law but for good and pressing social reasons, compels a suspected person to provide evidence against himself. It is, therefore, in our judgment, not surprising that a strict and compulsory code is laid down as a set of pre-conditions which must be fulfilled before any specimen produced by the defendant, which may condemn him at the hearing of the charge against him, can be adduced in evidence: no matter that there may be some instances where breach of the code occasions no discernible prejudice' (Watkins LJ in *Murray v DPP* [1993] RTR 209)

'A criminal trial is not a game under which a guilty defendant should be provided with a sporting chance. It is a search for truth in accordance with the twin principles that the prosecution must prove its case and that a defendant is not obliged to inculpate himself, the object being to convict the guilty and acquit the innocent. Requiring a defendant to indicate in advance what he disputes about the prosecution case offends neither of those principles' (*Gleeson* [2003] EWCA Crim 3357)

INTRODUCTION

10.1   For the advocate advising on drink/drug driving charges, there are two fundamental matters to consider. First, the admissibility of the specimen depends upon the adherence by the police to a strict and compulsory code when requiring a person to provide evidential specimens against themselves. Second, the advocate needs to identify at an early stage any failings in compliance with that code. It follows that the advocate must have a clear grasp of the law governing the admissibility of specimens for analysis.

10.2   Challenges to the procedure will come in the form of an application under section 78 of the Police and Criminal Evidence Act 1984 (PACE) for the court to exercise its discretion to refuse to allow evidence of the test results, if it appears to the court that, having regard to all the circumstances, including the circumstances in which the evidence was obtained, the admission of the evidence would have such an adverse effect on the fairness of the proceedings that the court ought not to admit it.

10.3   Drink or drug driving is typically detected when a police officer, having reasonable grounds, administers to the suspect one of three specific types of preliminary test: a preliminary breath test, a preliminary impairment test, or a preliminary drug test.

10.4   The evidence of the reading of these preliminary tests cannot replace the need for the evidential procedure. If the test is positive, the suspect is arrested and taken immediately to a police station where a request is made for an evidential specimen of breath, blood and/or urine. Breath is analysed by the police station Intoxilyzer machine; blood and urine are analysed by an authorised analyst. The suspect may additionally be assessed by a doctor or health care professional to determine if they are unfit through drink or drugs via an impairment test, or to allow the clinician to give an opinion to the officer on whether the suspect has a condition arising from the presence of drugs, enabling that officer to request a blood or urine sample. Subject to the results of these tests, the suspect may be charged and only released if they pass a final alcohol screening test.

10.5   A lawful arrest is not an essential prerequisite for the admissibility of the specimens, provided that they were obtained without inducement, threat, trick or other impropriety[1].

THE PRINCIPAL OFFENCES

10.6   There are three principal offences under the Road Traffic Act 1988 ('RTA 1988'):

(1)   Driving (or being in charge) with excess alcohol (s 5) or drugs (s 5A).

(2)   Driving (or being in charge) whilst unfit through drink or drugs (s 4).

(3)   Failing to provide a specimen (s 7).

1   *R v Fox* [1985] RTR 337; *Anderton v Royle* [1985] RTR 91).

EXCESS ALCOHOL

10.7   A person who drives or attempts to drive (or is in charge of) a motor vehicle on a road or other public place after consuming so much alcohol that the proportion of it in their breath, blood or urine exceeds the prescribed limit is guilty of an offence (RTA 1988, s 5).

'Excess' means above the prescribed limit, which is:

● 35 micrograms of alcohol in 100 millilitres of breath;

● 80 milligrammes of alcohol in 100 millilitres of blood; and

● 107 milligrammes of alcohol in 100 millilitres of urine.

EXCESS DRUGS

10.8   Section 5A of the RTA 1988 creates offences of driving or attempting to drive a motor vehicle, or of being in charge of a motor vehicle, on a road or other public place when there is a specified controlled drug in the body of the offender, and the proportion of the drug in their blood or urine exceeds the specified limit for that drug. A 'controlled drug' is any substance or product specified in Part I, II or III of Schedule 2 to the Misuse of Drugs Act 1971.

10.9   The limits are prescribed by the Drug Driving (Specified Limits) (England and Wales) Regulations 2014:

Controlled drug	Limit (microgrammes per litre of blood)
Amphetamine	250
Benzoylecgonine	50
Clonazepam	50
Cocaine	10
Delta-9-Tetrahydrocannabinol	2
Diazepam	550
Flunitrazepam	300
Ketamine	20
Lorazepam	100
Lysergic Acid Diethylamide	1
Methadone	500
Methylamphetamine	10
Methylenedioxymethamphetamine	10

Controlled drug	Limit (microgrammes per litre of blood)
6-Monoacetylmorphine	5
Morphine	80
Oxazepam	300
Temazepam	1000

10.10   A sample might indicate the presence of more than one drug. Given that a defendant may have a medical reason for one drug but not another, and there are different limits, there should be a separate charge for each drug found. Section 5A(3) of the RTA 1988 provides a defence if the drug was prescribed or supplied for medical purposes and taken in accordance with medical advice. Once raised, the prosecution must disprove this defence to the criminal standard.

BREATH PROCEDURE

10.11   The constable at the police station must first consider seeking a specimen of breath. Section 7(1)(a) of the RTA 1988 requires the suspect to provide two specimens of breath for analysis, and the specimen with the lower proportion of alcohol will be used evidentially.

10.12   The suspect is allowed three minutes in which to provide their first specimen and a further three minutes in which to provide a second specimen. According to the operator's handbook, up to five attempts should be possible in each three-minute period. The suspect must blow for a given interval at a given pressure. Whilst not required to blow hard, there must be continuous breath to complete the volume required. This is to ensure that the breath represents deep lung air.

10.13   The procedure conducted by the police officer will usually be captured evidentially in three ways:

- the officer conducting the procedure will complete a form contemporaneously (MG/DD forms);

- CCTV, body-worn footage, and audio footage from the Intoxilyzer room; and

- the specimen printout ('test record') produced by the Intoxilyzer.

BLOOD/URINE PROCEDURE AT THE STATION

10.14   The officer can seek blood or urine only if:

(a)   the officer believes breath cannot be provided for medical reasons,

(b)   the station breath machine is not working reliably,

(c)   the officer believes that the station breath machine has not produced a reliable result,

(d)   the officer believes the motorist has a drug in their body, or

(e)   the officer has been advised by a doctor or health care professional that the condition of the person might be due to a drug.

10.15   The specimen of blood must be taken by a doctor or health care professional. It is for the police officer to decide whether the specimen will be blood or urine. However, this is subject to the qualification that, if a medical reason is raised as to why a specimen of blood cannot or should not be taken, the issue is to be decided by a doctor or health care professional and not by the police officer.

10.16   Blood can be taken either with the suspect's true and unconditional consent at the time or, if incapable of consenting due to medical reasons, with the consent of a medical practitioner then and the suspect's consent later. The prosecution must prove that consent was given not only to the officer but also to the medical practitioner taking the blood[2]. In a later case, Lord Hutton set out what an officer must tell the driver when seeking to take blood at the station[3]:

> 'The requirements, which should be regarded as mandatory so that non-compliance should lead to an acquittal are … the warning as to the risk of prosecution required by section 7(7) [and] the statement of the reason under that subsection why breath specimens cannot be taken or used …'

> '…what is necessary is that the driver should be aware (whether or not he is told by the police officer) of the role of the doctor so that he does not suffer prejudice. Therefore, if the driver appreciates that a specimen of blood will be taken by a doctor and not by a police officer, the charge should not be dismissed by the justices because the police officer failed to tell the driver that the specimen would be taken by a doctor.'

URINE

10.17   'A specimen of urine must be provided within one hour of the request and after the provision of a previous specimen' (RTA 1988, s 7(5)). This procedure will usually be conducted in the cell where there is a latrine. The officer will

2   *Friel v Dickson* [1992] RTR 366.
3   *DPP v Jackson* [1998] 3 All ER 769.

explain the procedure and then hand the suspect a receptacle. The first sample of urine will be discarded, and the suspect will then be invited to provide a second sample for analysis.

10.18   There must be two distinct specimens given. Whilst the logic of a second sample is to ensure that fresh urine is subject to analysis, there is nothing in the statute or common law that requires the suspect to empty his bladder before giving the second sample, nor is there a requirement for the officer to wait a certain time before seeking that second sample[4]. However, if an officer tells the suspect to stop urinating and then to 'continue urinating' for the second sample, that will amount to one sample, not two[5].

10.19   The specimen of blood or urine taken will be divided into two: one part is sent for police laboratory analysis, and the other part is provided to the suspect *if requested*. The suspect will be given a leaflet as to what he must do with this sample to maintain its integrity. The police must ensure that it is stored, packaged and transported in the appropriate way. This is especially important in circumstances where cannabinoids are involved, as the breakdown rate is very fast.

HOSPITAL PATIENTS

10.20   Section 9 of the RTA 1988 provides protection for hospital patients. A 'hospital patient' cannot be required to provide breath but can be asked for blood or urine. However, the doctor in immediate charge must first be notified of the proposal to take the specimen. The doctor may object to not only the specimen being taken but also the 'requirement' being made if it would be prejudicial to the proper care and treatment of the patient.

10.21   It is not open to a patient to refuse a request for a specimen of blood because a previous sample was provided for hospital purposes[6].

10.22   If the suspect is incapable of consenting, section 7A of the RTA 1988 allows a request for blood to be made to a doctor, provided that:

(a)   the constable would have been entitled to request blood from the person but for the incapacity;

(b)   the suspect has been involved in an accident connected with the investigation;

---

4   *Over v Musker* [1985] RTR 84.
5   *Prosser v Dickeson* [1982] RTR 96.
6   *Kemp v CC of Kent* [1987] RTR 66.

(c)   it appears to the constable that the person is or may be incapable of giving valid consent to giving blood; and

(d)   it appears to the constable that the incapacity is attributable to medical reasons.

10.23   The request cannot be made to the doctor who has clinical care of the suspect. It will normally be made to a police doctor (or another doctor pressed into service, if necessary).

POST-INCIDENT CONSUMPTION OF ALCOHOL OR DRUGS; BACK-CALCULATION

10.24   The defendant can challenge the analysis if they prove that they consumed alcohol/drugs *after* the commission of the offence but before the analysis ('the hip-flask defence'). To determine this issue, the court must ask, 'but for the alcohol consumed after the offence, would the defendant have been over the limit at the time of the offence?'. This requires a 'back-calculation' from an expert, ie scientifically calculating the defendant's alcohol elimination rate and determining the contribution made by the additional alcohol to the eventual breath reading.

DRIVING OR ATTEMPTING TO DRIVE OR BEING IN CHARGE OF ANY MECHANICALLY PROPELLED VEHICLE WHILST UNFIT (RTA 1988, s 4)

10.25   Under section 4(1) of the RTA 1988, it is an offence if a person drives or attempts to drive any mechanically propelled vehicle (which includes any 'motor vehicle') on a road or other public place whilst unfit through drink or drugs. Similarly, section 4(2) of the RTA 1988 makes it an offence if the person is 'in charge' when under the influence of drink or drugs.

10.26   This offence is often prosecuted where there is evidence of impairment from alcohol/drugs *and* there is no reliable specimen available to enable a section 5 charge. 'Unfit' means that the ability to *drive properly is impaired*. Impairment may be judged from the erratic manner of driving, an accident occurring, the driver's presentation on body-worn video, and/or the results of a roadside breath test or a preliminary drug test. Whilst it is desirable that the prosecution call expert medical evidence of impairment from a doctor who examined the motorist in police custody, such evidence is not necessary[7]. A witness who is not an expert

---

7   *Leetham v DPP* [1999] RTR 29.

can only give his general impression of whether a person has taken a drink or drug. He cannot say whether that person was fit to drive[8].

10.27   The Road Traffic Offenders Act 1988 ('RTOA 1988') provides that any analysis of breath, blood or urine, whether above or below the limit, must be taken into account when determining impairment (RTOA 1988, s 15(2) and (3)). The lower the reading, the more favourable to the defence. The only exceptions to the use of such an analysis are when the analysis was obtained improperly or if the defendant can show that they consumed alcohol or drugs after the offence.

10.28   Causation must be proved. It must be shown that the impairment was *as a result of* the effect of the alcohol or drug, and that the alcohol or drug remained in the person's system at the time of driving[9].

10.29   It is not duplicitous to charge both sections 4 and 5 of the RTA 1988, but a plea to one will usually result in the withdrawal of the other. It may be more difficult for the prosecution to accept a charge under section 4 or 5 as an alternative to section 7 (Failing to provide), as the latter involves an element of obstruction of justice and has a higher starting point in the sentencing guidelines.

10.30   Where the police doctor conducting an impairment test concludes that the motorist's condition may be due to the influence of drugs, the police are entitled to request a specimen of blood or urine, depending on the type of drug suspected.

BEING IN CHARGE OF A VEHICLE WITH EXCESS ALCOHOL OR WHILST UNFIT

10.31   It is an offence to be *in charge* of a vehicle with excess alcohol. This caters for the stationary parked vehicle with a drunk motorist at the wheel and in circumstances where 'driving' cannot be proved. 'In charge' is not defined in the legislation and is very much a matter of fact and degree.

10.32   The question for the court is whether the motorist has assumed being in charge to the extent that they are in de facto control of the vehicle or, due the circumstances (eg in driver's seat, engine running), they might be expected to imminently assume control. However, it can also cater for a motorist not sitting in the vehicle. For example, an owner/possessor is prima facie *in charge* unless they put someone else in charge, or they ceased to be in actual control and there is no realistic possibility of their resuming actual control while unfit.

---

8   *Sherrard v Jacob* [1965]NI 151.
9   *R v Ealing Magistrates Court ex p Woodman* [1994] RTR 189.

10.33   The following factors need to be considered[10]:

(a)   whether and where they were in the vehicle or how far they were from it;

(b)   what they were doing at the relevant time;

(c)   whether they were in possession of a key that fitted the ignition;

(d)   whether there was evidence of an intention to take or assert control of the car by driving or otherwise; and

(e)   whether any person was in, at or near the vehicle and, if so, the like particulars of that person.

THE STATUTORY DEFENCE TO 'IN CHARGE' OR 'FORWARD-CALCULATIONS'

10.34   The prosecution does not need to prove that the defendant was *likely* to drive whilst in charge. However, there is a statutory defence if the defendant establishes that the circumstances were such that there was no likelihood of his driving the vehicle whilst the proportion of alcohol in his breath, blood or urine exceeded the prescribed limit (RTA 1988, s 5(2) or 4(3)). The burden of proof is on the defendant and the standard is on the balance of probabilities.

10.35   It is a common misconception that the key issue is the defendant's intention. Whilst their intentions form part of the picture, the issue is the actual likelihood of driving whilst over the limit. For example, a driver who plans to sleep off their drinking in the driver's seat may still be in charge, whereas a driver who intends to drive a car mechanically incapable of being driven due to an engine fault may not be in charge.

10.36   To determine this issue, the court will commonly need to know how long the motorist would have remained over the legal limit. This will require a 'forward-calculation' from an expert, ie scientifically calculating the defendant's alcohol elimination rate and looking forward in time to determine when they would cease to be over the limit.

FAILING TO PROVIDE A SPECIMEN (RTA 1988, s 7)

10.37   Failing or refusing, without 'reasonable excuse', to provide a specimen when required is an offence. What is a reasonable excuse? The court will approach the issue in two steps[11]:

---

10   *DPP v Watkins* [1989] 2 WLR 966.
11   *Law v Stephens* [1971] RTR 358.

10.38   *Drink/drug driving*

(1)   Is the excuse capable in law of amounting to a reasonable excuse?

(2)   If so, whether it is in fact a reasonable excuse is a matter of fact and degree.

10.38   Justices should take great care not to be gullible in accepting medical reasons as a reasonable excuse[12]. Evidence will normally be required from a medical practitioner of the inability although, in some circumstances, it could come from the defendant alone[13].

10.39   Where a suspect claims to have medical reasons for not providing a sample of breath, the officer must:

(1)   decide as a layperson whether the claim is capable of being such a condition; there may be many cases in which a constable, faced with what appears to be a bogus or imaginative assertion of a medical condition, may, after proper consideration, respond with a terse negative and proceed to require two specimens of breath; and

(2)   if the claim is capable of being such a condition, consider whether they have reasonable cause to believe that, as a consequence of that condition, breath cannot be provided or should not be required (causation).

10.40   If an officer proceeds prematurely to charge a suspect with failing to provide, either through an unreasonable assessment of the medical explanation or a failure to exercise the discretion at all, the procedure may be challenged as inadmissible.

10.41   Provided there was sufficient material to justify the officer's decision that the reason asserted by the suspect gave them reasonable cause to believe in the existence of medical reasons for not requiring a specimen of breath, the decision was the constable's alone and they are not required to summon a doctor to give an opinion.

10.42   Where, however, there was no reason for not choosing urine in preference to blood, and a valid reason was put forward as to why urine should be the choice instead of blood, the officer must at least consider whether blood or urine should be the choice. Therefore, if the officer concluded that the required specimen should be the one to which the motorist objected, without any basis for doing so, the decision could be seen as perverse. Alternatively, it could be said that the officer had misunderstood the legal position and the statutory procedure had not been followed, and that the police officer, in exercising their discretion

---

12   *Watkins LJ in DPP v Eddowes* [1991] RTR 35.
13   *Grady v Pollard* [1988] RTR 316.

before coming to their conclusion to require blood, should have considered the defendant's genuine belief that they should not give a blood sample[14].

10.43   Where there is any doubt in the mind of the officer, they should call a doctor or health care professional. It has been held that, when a driver refused blood because he took tablets, the officer should not have dismissed the answer out of hand and should have asked further questions, considered the matter properly, and asked a doctor if in doubt[15]:

> 'The prosecutor had to establish that the defendant's statement about taking tablets was incapable of amounting to a medical reason; that, in the absence of evidence before the justices that the sergeant took into account, or gave consideration to whether, the defendant's statement about taking tablets should be treated as a medical reason, the justices erred in holding that he had performed the correct procedure laid down in section 7 of the Road Traffic Act of 1988.'

10.44   It has been said that a reasonable excuse 'must arise out of a physical or mental inability to provide one, or a substantial risk to health in its provision'[16]. The following have all been advanced, and either accepted or dismissed, as reasonable excuses:

- An invincible repugnance to hypodermic needles may be a reasonable excuse.

- Relying on the advice of a solicitor to refuse to provide a sample is not a reasonable excuse[17].

- Trying to delay the procedure to obtain legal advice is not a reasonable excuse[18].

- Doing one's best and making every effort is not a reasonable excuse in the absence of evidence of some inability.

However:

- A suspect who loses confidence in a doctor after three unsuccessful attempts to obtain blood may have a reasonable excuse[19].

- It is a reasonable excuse if the suspect was unable to understand, because of their limited command of English, the purpose of the requirement to

---

14   *Joseph v DPP* [2004] R.T.R. 21.
15   *Wade v DPP* [1996] R.T.R. 177.
16   *R v Lennard* [1973] RTR 252.
17   *Dickinson v DPP* [1989] Crim LR 741.
18   *CPS v Chalupa* [2009] EWHC 3082 (Admin).
19   *R v Harling* [1970] RTR 441.

provide a sample or the consequences of a failure/refusal[20]. Now that every police station has access to Language line, a telephone translating service, this excuse is unlikely to succeed.

10.45   The burden of proof is on the prosecution, to the criminal standard once reasonable excuse has been raised by the defendant. The comment of Stephenson LJ[21] is a useful guide as to what must be evidentially presented to meet the threshold for reasonable excuse:

> 'We wish to make it plain that our decision does not mean that the appellant had a reasonable excuse or that other motorists can hope to avoid conviction … by the simple expedient of claiming that they were too frightened of the needle to give a specimen of blood, without any medical evidence as to their mental state. The law expects responsible adults to overcome their fears, whether rational or irrational, in order to comply with it. The mental condition or physical injuries of one who refuses to provide a specimen … "must be of a very extreme character to constitute a reasonable excuse" – and that applies, in our judgment, to a mental condition alleged to result from a nervous constitution or from a traumatic experience in the past. No fear short of a phobia recognized by medical science to be as strong and inhibiting as, for instance, claustrophobia can be allowed to excuse failure to provide a specimen for a laboratory test, and in most if not all cases where the fear of providing it is claimed to be invincible the claim will have to be supported by medical evidence.'

THE MG/DD FORMS

10.46   Completed during the sample procedure, the Manual of Guidance Drink and Drug driving 'MG/DD') forms are intended as a 'layperson's guide' to the operation of the drink and drug drive laws. Failure to comply with the guidance is not fatal, provided the law is complied with. Not every error in the procedure will result in the exclusion of the evidential sample.

10.47   The advocate should have particular regard to:

1.   In section 4 unfit prosecutions, the description of the manner of the suspect.

2.   In section 4 unfit prosecutions, did the officer contemplate investigating impairment at the time?

---

20   *Beck v Sager* [1979] Crim LR 257; *CC of Avon & Somerset v Singh* [1988] RTR 107.
21   *R. v Harding* [1974] RTR 325.

3. Whether the suspect told the officer about any post-driving consumption or consumption of an 'interfering substance'.

4. Was the suspect was warned about the risk of prosecution? A failure to properly warn will be fatal to both a prosecution for section 7 (Failing to provide) and section 5 (Excess alcohol)[22].

5. Was the warning of the risk of prosecution understood if the suspect had cognitive difficulties or a limited command of English (see *Chief Constable of Avon & Somerset v Singh* [1988] RTR 107 above)?

6. In 'failing to provide' cases, whether the officer asked for medical reasons and, if so, the suspect's reply.

7. Where medical reasons were given but not believed, the notes, if any, which the officer made of his decision-making process.

8. Whether the specimen printout shows that the Intoxilyzer was properly calibrated before and after the evidential sample with a simulator check of 35 μgs of alcohol.

9. In 'failing to provide' cases, whether the volume of breath provided (as shown on the test record) was consistent with a genuine attempt to provide.

10. In section 5 excess alcohol cases, whether the breath analysis readings properly reflect the reading in the charge.

11. Whether the gap between the lower and higher sample of breath is greater than 15%.

12. Whether any additional comments of the suspect, or events outside the scope of the form, were properly recorded by the officer.

SENTENCING

10.48 Where a person is convicted of an offence involving obligatory disqualification, the court must order them to be disqualified for a period of at least 12 months, unless the court (for special reasons) thinks fit to order them to be disqualified for a shorter period or not to order them to be disqualified (RTOA 1988, s 34(1)).

10.49 Thus, the starting position is that a conviction for *driving* with excess alcohol, driving whilst unfit, or failing to provide a specimen carries obligatory endorsement and disqualification for at least 12 months. This increases to at least two years if the offender has had two or more disqualifications for periods of 56

---

22 *Murray v DPP* [1993] RTR 209.

days or more in the preceding three years, and further increases to at least three years if the offender has been convicted of a relevant drink-driving offence in the preceding 10 years.

10.50   Where the court imposes a custodial sentence as well as a driving ban, the court must extend the length of the ban by half the custodial term (Sentencing Act 2020, s 166). This is on the basis that a defendant will be released halfway through their sentence, so the driving ban will cover the half of the sentence served on licence, and then the full driving ban on top of that. This avoids a period of the driving ban being served whilst in custody.

10.51   A conviction for being *in charge* with excess alcohol, in charge whilst unfit, or 'failing to provide' (in charge) carries a discretionary disqualification. If no disqualification is imposed, the court must impose 10 penalty points.

SPECIAL REASONS

10.52   It is open to the court to find that, due to the circumstances of the offence, there are special reasons not to disqualify or to reduce the length of the disqualification. The minimum criteria for what amounts to special reasons was set out as follows[23].

The reason must be:

(a)   a mitigating or extenuating circumstance;

(b)   not amount to a defence in law;

(c)   be directly connected to the commission of the offence; and

(d)   one which the court ought properly to take into consideration.

10.53   In the context of drink-driving, the most frequent examples of special reasons are the shortness of distance driven, a genuine emergency, or where the drinks have been laced. It should be noted that the greater the alcohol level, the less likely the court will find special reasons. In a case concerned with dealing with an emergency, it was said that[24]:

> 'if the alcohol content in the defendant's body is very high, that is a very powerful reason for saying that the discretion should not be exercised in his favour. Indeed if the alcohol content exceeds 100 milligrammes per 100 millilitres of blood, the justices should rarely, if ever, exercise this discretion in favour of the driver.'

---

23   *R v Wickins* (1958) 42 Cr.App.R. 236.
24   *Taylor v Rajan* [1974] 1 All ER 1087.

REDUCTION OF DISQUALIFICATION

10.54   A court will typically offer the drink-driving offender an opportunity to complete a rehabilitation course for drink-driver offenders. If completed, this will reduce the length of the disqualification by up to 25%. This scheme is not currently available for excess drug offenders.

SUSPENSION OF DISQUALIFICATION PENDING APPEAL

10.55   Section 39(1) of the RTOA 1988 permits a court to suspend a disqualification pending appeal 'if it thinks fit'.

REMOVAL OF DISQUALIFICATION

10.56   Section 42 of the RTOA 1988 allows an offender to apply for the early removal of the disqualification:

- if the driving ban is less than four years, after two years;

- if the ban is between four and 10 years, at the halfway point; and

- for any ban for 10 years or longer, after five years.

Accordingly, a person banned for two years or less cannot apply for early removal.

Chapter 11

Careless driving

Nick Lee

INTRODUCTION

11.1   The offence of careless or inconsiderate driving is set out in section 3 of the Road Traffic Act 1988 ('RTA 1988'):

'If a person drives a mechanically propelled vehicle on a road or other public place without due care and attention, or without reasonable consideration for other persons using the road or place, he is guilty of an offence.'

11.2   Pre-1988, case law had established the test for liability as whether a person was exercising the degree of care and attention that a reasonable and prudent driver would exercise in the circumstances. It is accepted that this is essentially the same test, and pre-1988 case law is good law.

11.3   An amendment to the RTA 1988 was enacted in 2006 to provide further clarity. Section 3ZA defines driving 'without due care and attention' or 'without reasonable consideration':

'[...]

(2)   A person is to be regarded as driving without due care and attention if (and only if) the way he drives falls below what would be expected of a competent and careful driver.

(3)   In determining for the purposes of subsection (2) above what would be expected of a careful and competent driver in a particular case, regard shall be had not only to the circumstances of which he could be expected to be aware but also to any circumstances shown to have been within the knowledge of the accused.

(4)   A person is to be regarded as driving without reasonable consideration for other persons only if those persons are inconvenienced by his driving.'

11.4   Section 1 of the RTA 1988 applies to careless driving, such that a driver cannot normally be convicted unless he was warned at the time the offence was committed that he may be prosecuted, or a summons or a Notice of Intended Prosecution was served on him within 14 days of the offence. There are a number of exceptions to this limitation period, however, and detailed research will be needed where a prosecution appears to fall foul of it.

11.5   Careless driving is a summary offence and will usually be dealt with in the magistrates' court. A defendant charged with dangerous driving in the Crown Court can plead guilty to careless driving, and a jury can convict of careless driving as an alternative. There may be good tactical reasons to leave the alternative to the jury.

ELEMENTS OF THE OFFENCE

11.6   Driving is defined as being at the controls of a vehicle for the purposes of controlling its movement, whether it is moving or stationary with the engine running, even for a short period of time. Sitting in grid-locked traffic with the engine running therefore counts as 'driving'. The meaning of 'mechanically propelled vehicle' and 'road or other public place' are discussed elsewhere in this book.

11.7   Once those facts are established, a defendant can commit the offence in two ways:

(i)   their driving fell below what would be expected of a competent and careful driver; or

(ii)   they drove without reasonable consideration for other road users.

11.8   The broad language of the statute makes the offence applicable to a wide range of circumstances and adaptable to changes in technology, transport habits and expectations, but the drafting has been criticised for establishing a low bar for criminal liability and leaving the public without a clear definition of what is required by a competent and careful driver. Every driver fails to meet this standard sometimes, if not regularly.

11.9   A similar angle of criticism has been that the offence criminalises negligence, which is criminalised elsewhere only in extreme circumstances, such as manslaughter. An independent review commissioned by the Department of

Transport prior to the enactment of the RTA 1988 questioned why it is an offence to drive a car without due care and attention, even when no injury or damage is caused, but it is not an offence to injure someone by using a chainsaw negligently. The report noted, however, that thousands of deaths and injuries occur on the roads each year and justified the criminalisation of careless driving by way of comparison with the criminalisation of health and safety breaches.

11.10   It is for the prosecution to prove to the criminal standard that a defendant is guilty. The offence is committed if the driver's actions fall below the required standard. No damage or injury needs to be caused. If the defendant's actions may have been consistent with those of a competent and careful driver, he should be acquitted.

Driving that falls below the level of a competent or careful driver

11.11   The Court of Appeal has described the 'competent and careful driver' test as[1]:

'[…] an objective standard, impersonal and universal, fixed in relation to the safety of other road users of the highway. It is in no way related to the degree of proficiency or degree of experience attained by the individual driver.'

11.12   This means that a defendant's personal characteristics and driving experience are irrelevant when evaluating whether their driving fell below the required standard. A learner driver is judged according to the same objective standard as a police driver responding to an emergency[2]. The question is whether their actions or omissions fell below what would be expected of a competent and careful driver in the same circumstances. It is unhelpful to complicate this question of fact by introducing concepts such as 'error of judgment'[3].

11.13   A driver suddenly faced with an emergency should not be judged with the benefit of hindsight. The question is whether it was reasonable for them to have acted as they did at the time[4]. The offence can be committed in an infinite number of ways. The Highway Code can assist in demonstrating that a defendant's driving did or did not fall below the required standard, but a breach of the code does not necessarily mean the driving was careless in law.

1   *McCrone v Riding* [1938] 1 All ER 157.
2   *R v Bannister (Craig)* [2009] EWCA Crim 1571.
3   *Simpson v Peat* [1952] 2 QB 24.
4   *R v Bristol Crown Court, ex parte Jones* [1986] RTR 259.

11.14   *Careless driving*

11.14   The CPS website lists a number of examples of what might amount to careless driving:

(i)   Overtaking on the inside.

(ii)   Driving inappropriately close to another vehicle.

(iii)   Inadvertently driving through a red light.

(iv)   Emerging from a side road into the path of another vehicle.

(v)   Tuning a car radio when the driver was avoidably distracted by this action.

(vi)   Using a hand-held mobile phone when the driver was avoidably distracted by that use – this now carries a mandatory six penalty points as a standalone offence.

(vii)   Selecting and lighting a cigarette or similar when the driver was avoidably distracted by that action.

These are indicative only and each case will turn on its own facts. Opinion evidence as to a defendant's speed may be admissible, even if such evidence would be insufficient to found a conviction for speeding.

11.15   The physical condition of the driver is relevant. For example, a court can conclude that a competent and careful driver would not drive after suffering a head injury[5]. Evidence that the defendant had been drinking alcohol before driving is admissible if relevant to the standard of driving, even if there is no charge relating to driving with excess alcohol. The court may be persuaded to exclude such evidence, however, under section 78 of the Police and Criminal Evidence Act 1984 ('PACE').

11.16   There may be no direct evidence of the standard of driving but the factual matrix is such that the only realistic explanation for what happened is that the defendant drove carelessly. For example, on a dry day, in a 30mph zone, he left the road and collided with a phone box. The prosecution does not have to negative every possible explanation for the accident but, once the defendant advances an explanation for what happened (eg he swerved to avoid an oncoming vehicle which had drifted on to his side of the road, or a sudden mechanical defect of which he had no warning), the prosecution must prove that explanation is untrue to the criminal standard. The court should not speculate or theorise about why a defendant acted as he did without an evidential basis. For example, a court wrongly acquitted a motorcyclist when deciding that he must have experienced a dizzy spell or been hit by a stone or bird when that explanation was not in evidence[6].

---

5   *Jones (Adrian) v CPS* [2019] EWHC 2826 (Admin).
6   *Oakes v Foster* [1961] 1 WLUK 428.

11.17   There is no express mens rea and the prosecution does not have to prove that a defendant was aware of the consequences of his actions or omissions. Defences of automatism, duress of circumstances or insanity may apply. Section 3ZA(2) of the RTA 1988 directs the court to have regard to any circumstances shown to have been within the defendant's personal knowledge. This will usually count against the defendant. For example, a defendant who knows their steering is defective can be convicted for a manoeuvre that was careless because he knew his vehicle had a tendency to drift to the left, or a defendant's knowledge that he is subject to hypoglycaemic attacks may be admissible[7]. There is arguably some unfairness in taking account of such circumstances when they count against the defendant but not, for example, when they can demonstrate an advanced driving qualification as part of their training as a police pursuit driver, but that is the settled position in case law[8].

Driving without reasonable consideration for other persons

11.18   The offence can also be committed when a defendant fails to show reasonable consideration for other persons using the road. Here, the prosecution has to show that other persons were inconvenienced by the defendant's driving. This might be the appropriate charge where the defendant has, for example, forced another driver off the road by flashing their lights, or deliberately driven through a puddle to soak pedestrians. It must be the defendant's driving which is at fault, so shouting from the car window will not suffice.

SENTENCE

11.19   Careless or inconsiderate driving is punishable by way of a fine (no maximum) and penalty points or discretionary disqualification. The Sentencing Council has published Guidelines for careless driving[9]. As with all Sentencing Guidelines, these are guidelines rather than tramlines.

11.20   The Sentencing Guidelines set out three categories of offence depending on whether features of greater culpability and/or greater harm are present. Category 1 is the most serious and Category 3 is the least serious. It would be unusual for there to be no features of greater culpability or greater harm but for the incident to still have been spotted and deemed worthy of prosecution, so the question most often will be whether the case falls into Category 1 or 2:

---

7   *R v Marison* [1997] RTR 457.
8   *R v Bannister (Craig)* [2009] EWCA Crim 1571 overruled *Milton v CPS* [2007] EWHC 532 (Admin) on this point.
9   The current version became effective on 24 April 2017.

11.21 *Careless driving*

(a)   Category 3 cases are sentenced by way of a Band A fine and 3–4 penalty points.

(b)   Category 2 offences are sentenced by way of a Band B fine and 5–6 penalty points.

(c)   Category 1 offences are sentenced by way of a Band C fine and 7–9 points or discretionary disqualification.

(d)   A case which falls into Category 2 under a strict application of the Sentencing Guidelines may be elevated to Category 1 if, for example, the level of injury suffered is too serious for the case to remain in Category 2.

11.21   The imposition of penalty points can result in a disqualification under the 'totting up' provisions, so, if defending, you should find out how many points the defendant has on their licence and be ready to make an exceptional hardship argument at sentence, if one is warranted. You should also consider in advance whether there are special reasons not to disqualify, or to disqualify for a shorter period of time, and be prepared to make that argument at sentence, if it is appropriate.

11.22   Where you intend to advance arguments such as exceptional hardship or special reasons, you should put the prosecution and court on notice as soon as you can, and consider whether any prosecution witnesses need to be warned for sentence and what evidence the defendant might be able to provide to support your application.

APPEAL

11.23   Careless driving is a summary offence so the avenues of appeal will usually be an appeal against conviction or sentence to the Crown Court (for a full re-run of the trial or sentencing exercise), or an appeal by way of case stated or judicial review to the High Court. The High Court will only interfere with the magistrates' decision if satisfied that no reasonable court could have concluded that the driving fell below the required standard.

Chapter 12

Dangerous driving

David Scutt

12.1   A chapter on dangerous driving could be a very long one. There is a plethora of case law but this chapter is, deliberately, a summary of the most important aspects of dangerous driving because, as a matter of common sense, every case of alleged dangerous driving will be fact-specific. The offence can be committed in a large number of different ways.

Section 2 of the Road Traffic Act 1988 ('RTA 1988') provides:

'A person who drives a mechanically propelled vehicle dangerously on a road or other public place is guilty of an offence.'

Section 2A of the RTA 1988 provides:

'2A Meaning of dangerous driving.

(1)   For the purposes of sections 1[1], 1A[2] and 2 [RTA 1988] a person is to be regarded as driving dangerously if (and, subject to subsection (2) below, only if)–

(a)   the way he drives falls far below what would be expected of a competent and careful driver, and

(b)   it would be obvious to a competent and careful driver that driving in that way would be dangerous.

(2)   A person is also to be regarded as driving dangerously for the purposes of sections 1, 1A and 2 [RTA 1988] if it would be obvious to a competent and careful driver that driving the vehicle in its current state would be dangerous.

(3)   In subsections (1) and (2) above "dangerous" refers to danger either of injury to any person or of serious damage to property; and in determining for the purposes of these subsections what would be expected of, or obvious to, a competent and careful

---

1   Causing Death by Dangerous Driving.
2   Causing Serious Injury by Dangerous Driving.

driver in a particular case, regard shall be had not only to the circumstances of which he could be expected to be aware but also to any circumstances shown to have been within the knowledge of the accused.

(4) In determining for the purposes of subsection (2) above the state of a vehicle, regard may be had to anything attached to or carried on or in it and to the manner in which it is attached or carried.'

ELEMENTS

'A person'

12.2   'A person' means an actual person and not a company[3].

'Drives'

12.3   The test for whether a person was driving a vehicle is whether they were, in a substantial sense, controlling the movement and direction of the vehicle, and the activity must fall within the ordinary meaning of the word 'drive'. Whether someone was 'driving' in the ordinary sense of the word is a question of fact and degree.

'Dangerously'

12.4   The test to be applied when considering what amounts to dangerous driving is purely objective, concentrating on the nature of the driving.

It is a two-limbed test:

(1) the standard of driving must fall 'far below what would be expected of a competent and careful driver'; and

(2) the dangerousness of the driving must be 'obvious to a competent and careful driver'.

12.5   The fact that a driver might have special skills (such as advanced police drivers) is not relevant to the assessment of whether driving was dangerous, because the objective standard to be applied is that of 'a competent and careful driver'[4]. It follows that a lack of skill and/or inexperience will also be irrelevant to that assessment. Such matters may go to mitigation.

---

3   *Richmond LBC v Pinn and Wheeler Ltd* [1989] RTR 354, DC.
4   Eg *R v Craig Bannister* [2009] EWCA Crim 1571.

12.6   Mistake of fact is irrelevant – for example, where a police officer in a marked police car drove through a red light during the pursuit of a stolen car in the mistaken belief that other police officers were controlling the junction[5]. Such matters may be relevant to mitigation, but do not amount to a defence.

12.7   Evidence relating to the condition of the driver can be considered under section 2A(3). The impact of drink and drugs are obvious. Drivers suffering from diabetes[6] and epilepsy[7] can be held to have driven dangerously if, being aware of their condition, they fail to medicate. It would be sensible to obtain expert evidence on the *actual* impact of alcohol, drugs and/or 'untreated' medical conditions; assumptions should not be made and may be very wrong. Going without sleep for a long period and then driving is another factor often taken into account, and it is the responsibility of the driver to ensure that they are in a fit state to drive.

12.8   The dangerous state of the vehicle (s 2A(2)) must be 'obvious to a careful and competent driver'. 'Obvious' is an ordinary English word with no special meaning and requiring no further judicial definition[8].

12.9   The dangerous state should be something that could be 'seen or realised at first glance'[9]. This means that, if the state of the vehicle is not obviously dangerous to a competent and careful driver, and the driver has no particular knowledge of the state of the vehicle, no offence is committed, however dangerous the vehicle may actually be. However, if the defendant has chosen to drive a vehicle which he knows to be in a dangerous condition (even though that defect would not be obvious to anyone else), he could be convicted on the basis of his knowledge. This introduces an element of subjectivity into what is usually an objective test, although it may be difficult for the prosecution to prove.

12.10   The words 'current state' ins 2A(2) imply a different state to the vehicle's 'original' or 'manufactured' state – that is, a lack of maintenance or positive alteration[10].

12.11   The following is a (non-exhaustive) list of examples of driving behaviour likely to be charged as dangerous driving[11]:

5   *Collins (L)* [1997] RTR 439, CA.
6   *Marison* [1997] RTR 457, CA.
7   *Lowe* [1997] 2 Cr App R (S) 324, CA and *Akinyeme* [2007] EWCA Crim 3290.
8   *Marsh* [2002] EWCA Crim 137.
9   *Strong* [1995] Crim LR 428, CA.
10   *Marchant* [2003] EWCA Crim 2099.
11   Derived from a combination of 'The Crown Prosecution Service Charging Practice for Dangerous Driving' and 'The Definitive Guideline for Causing Death by Dangerous Driving'.

- Aggressive driving (such as sudden lane changes or cutting into a line of vehicles or driving much too close to the vehicle in front).

- Racing or competitive driving.

- Speed that is highly inappropriate for the prevailing road or traffic conditions.

- Disregard of traffic lights and other road signs which, on an objective analysis, would appear to be deliberate.

- Failing to have a proper and safe regard for vulnerable road users such as cyclists, motorcyclists, horse riders, the elderly and pedestrians or when in the vicinity of a pedestrian crossing, hospital, school or residential home.

- Overtaking which could not have been carried out safely.

- Disregard of warnings from fellow passengers.

- Driving a vehicle knowing it has a dangerous defect or is poorly maintained or with a load which presents a danger to other road users.

- Using a hand-held mobile phone or other hand-held electronic equipment when the driver is avoidably and dangerously distracted by that use.

- Driving whilst avoidably and dangerously distracted, such as whilst reading a newspaper/map, talking to and looking at a passenger, selecting and lighting a cigarette, or by adjusting the controls of electronic equipment such as a radio, hands-free mobile phone or satellite navigation equipment.

- Driving when knowingly suffering from a medical or physical condition that significantly and dangerously impairs the offender's driving skills, such as having an arm or leg in plaster, or impaired eyesight. It can include the failure to take prescribed medication.

- Driving when knowingly deprived of adequate sleep or rest.

- A brief but obvious danger arising from a seriously dangerous manoeuvre. This covers situations where a driver has made a mistake or an error of judgement that was so substantial that it caused the driving to be dangerous even for only a short time.

'Road or other public place'

12.12   What is meant by a road or other public place is covered in more detail in Chapter 2. Section 192(1) of the RTA 1988 defines 'road' as 'any highway and any other road to which the public has access and includes bridges over which a road passes'. There is no definition of 'public place'.

12.13 A 'road' has been defined as a definable right of way for passage between two points[12]. Whether something is a road, highway or public place is a question of fact and degree, and the onus is on the prosecution to prove that a road or public place comes within the definition.

12.14 'The public' refers to the general public and not to some restricted class of person, and 'access' would generally mean unrestricted access (for the purposes of a 'road'). There must be sufficient evidence of the use of a place by the general public for it to be established to be a public place. Again, this is a matter of fact and degree.

THE DIFFERENCE BETWEEN DANGEROUS AND CARELESS DRIVING

12.15 In simple terms, the difference between dangerous and careless driving is the extent to which the driving falls below that which would be expected of a competent and careful driver. For dangerous driving, the standard must fall 'far below', as opposed to 'below'.

12.16 It is not infrequent in a case of 'causing death by dangerous driving' for the appellant to assert that the correct charge should be 'causing death by careless driving'. Whilst there is often an overlap between the lower end of dangerous driving and the upper end of careless driving, the driving in one case, which involved momentarily pushing the accelerator rather than the brake whilst in a state of panic, was deemed to be capable of being dangerous[13].

12.17 In cases where your client accepts the other elements of the offence, and the nature of the driving is on the borderline between dangerous and careless, it is always worth canvassing a plea to the lesser offence with the prosecutor. They may well be tempted to accept a plea to careless driving where there are some doubts as to whether the driving can genuinely be characterised as dangerous. Where a defendant is on trial in the Crown Court for dangerous driving, the jury can convict them of the lesser alternative of careless driving.

ALLOCATION

12.18 Under the Road Traffic Offenders Act 1988 ('RTOA 1988'), dangerous driving is triable either way (RTOA 1988, s 9 and Sch. 2, Pt I).

---

12 *Oxford v Austin* [1981] RTR 416.
13 *R v Shearing* [2012] EWCA Crim 842.

ALTERNATIVE VERDICTS

12.19 Section 3 of the RTA 1988 covers the offence of careless/inconsiderate driving.

SENTENCING

12.20 It is very common for dangerous driving prosecutions to originate in a blue-light police pursuit. When opening a case for sentence as a prosecutor, it helps to have the following:

- A route of the chase, normally provided by the police.

- An understanding of the risk to the public: was the defendant driving at high speed past a school when many children were around, or was it 4am on an empty country road?

- Duration of the dangerous driving: how long were the police following the defendant for?

- Body-worn video footage or dash-cam footage, which will show not only the route but also the speed and timing.

12.21 The maximum sentence for dangerous driving is two years' imprisonment. The court must also endorse the driver's licence and disqualify for at least 12 months. An extended re-test is also mandatory before the driving licence can be restored. If the offender has had two or more disqualifications for periods of 56 days or more in the three years preceding the date of the offence, the court must disqualify for a minimum of two years.

12.22 Despite the relatively low maximum sentence, custodial sentences are not uncommon in cases of dangerous driving, especially when the offence is combined (as is often the case) with other offences such as a lack of insurance, failing to stop, or driving whilst disqualified. Cases in which other road users had to take evasive action, or where the course of driving culminated in a collision, tend to result in heavier sentences.

12.23 At the time of writing, there are no sentencing guidelines for use in the Crown Court. However, a consultation guideline is currently being considered by the Sentencing Council. There are guidelines for the magistrates' court[14.]

---

14 www.sentencingcouncil.org.uk/offences/magistrates-court/item/dangerous-driving.

Chapter 13

Wanton or furious driving

George Joseph

13.1   The somewhat anachronistic offence of wanton or furious driving is possibly the oldest driving offence on the statute books. Despite its vintage, it is a useful offence as it covers a range of scenarios which are not catered for by the provisions of the Road Traffic Act 1988 ('RTA 1988').

DEFINITION

13.2   The offence is codified under section 35 of the Offences Against the Person Act 1861: 'Whosoever, having the charge of any carriage or vehicle, shall by wanton or furious driving or racing, or other wilful misconduct, or by wilful neglect, do or cause to be done any bodily harm to any person whatsoever, shall be guilty of an offence ...'.

13.3   The offence under section 35 is most often used today to deal with off-road drivers of motorised vehicles, horse-drawn carriages, and bicycles when they cannot be prosecuted for dangerous driving or cycling because their conduct did not take place on a road or a public highway. The offence has received some recent coverage in cases where cyclists have mounted the pavement and collided with pedestrians. This has resulted in serious injuries and, in some cases, death.

13.4   The offence is triable on indictment only, meaning that it must be dealt with in the Crown Court.

ELEMENTS OF THE OFFENCE

Being in charge of any carriage or vehicle

13.5   The 1861 Act refers to 'carriages', meaning horse-drawn carriages, though this now encompasses both motorised and non-motorised vehicles, including bicycles, scooters and segways. Unlike dangerous or careless driving, this is an offence which is not limited to public roads. In *R v Cooke*[1], the defendant was found guilty of wanton and furious driving after driving a van recklessly on a recreation ground and causing injury. As cycling and electric scooters grow ever more popular, this seemingly antiquated offence may become increasingly relevant.

13.6   What is meant by being 'in charge' of a vehicle is considered in depth in Chapter 10.

Wanton or furious driving or racing

13.7   Do not be perturbed by the archaic language; the term 'wanton' should be given its ordinary meaning which, in this context, means to drive irresponsibly, erratically, or simply badly. In *R v Knight*[2], the Court of Appeal found that 'wanton' was meant to be taken as being essentially reckless, involving the defendant 'driving in such a manner as to create an obvious and serious risk of causing physical harm to some other person who might be using the road …'.

13.8   It should be noted that the offence can be committed in two ways: either by 'wanton or furious driving' or by racing. Racing – even if done carefully (eg around the M25 in the middle of the night) – can amount to this offence, in addition to the obvious potential for a speeding ticket.

Wilful misconduct, or by wilful neglect

13.9   Wilful misconduct or wilful neglect is not to be construed as requiring a defendant to intend to cause bodily harm. All the prosecution are required to prove is that the nature of the wanton and furious driving was intentional, that it fell below the standard of a reasonable driver, and that the driving caused the injury which amounts to bodily harm. A better and more modern word which would cover this rather obscure phrase would be 'negligence'; lack of foresight or consideration for other road users is sufficient.

13.10   In *Cooke*[3], the judge directed the jury that 'misconduct' had its normal meaning and that it was up to the jury themselves to decide whether the driver's conduct fell below the reasonable standard of driving, so as to be deemed

---

1   [1971] Crim LR 44.
2   [2004] EWCA Crim 2998.
3   *R v Cooke* [1971] Crim LR 44.

misconduct. Obviously, each case would be considered on its own merits, but the following factors should be considered:

(a)　The type of vehicle being driven. There are a number of cases involving 'fixed gear' bikes which have no brakes. These bikes require the rider to reverse the pedals to slow down, or use their legs to brake. Plainly, mounting the pavement at speed could be considered wilful misconduct.

(b)　The speed of the vehicle being driven. This will be an issue for the jury to determine in the circumstances of each case. What is reasonable in some circumstances will be wholly unreasonable in others, and will always depend upon the precise factors of an individual case.

(c)　Any attempt to stop the vehicle. The driver may try to reduce their speed or bring their driving back to the standard of a normal driver, but if the damage has already taken place, this could only really go to mitigate the offence and reduce a driver's culpability.

(d)　Contextual factors. What was the weather like? Did the injured party contribute to the incident in any way? Was the driver inebriated in any way? Was the wilful misconduct only for a short period of time?

Bodily harm

13.11　In the context of this offence, to cause bodily harm requires the defendant to have driven or operated some form of vehicle (whether a car, horse-drawn carriage, bicycle etc) and to have caused actual bodily harm (ABH). Actual bodily harm includes any hurt or injury which interferes with the health or comfort of the victim. These injuries can include, but are not limited to, cuts, bruises or even losing consciousness. The injuries do not need to be grave or permanent but must be more than superficial or transient. Bodily harm does not include mere emotions such as fear, distress and panic. There needs to be actual injury for there to be bodily harm. However, harm that amounts to a recognised psychiatric illness can amount to actual bodily harm, but this needs to be proved by medical evidence.

SENTENCING RANGE

13.12　The offence itself carries a maximum sentence of two years' imprisonment and/or a fine. If convicted of this offence, the driver's licence will be endorsed with between three and nine penalty points.

13.13　Disqualification, which is obligatory in respect of mechanical vehicles, can also be imposed for other vehicles under section 28 of the Road Safety Act

2006, but this is at the court's discretion. This means that a defendant found guilty of wanton and furious driving when using a bicycle can be disqualified from driving a car. This is precisely what happened in the case of *R v Darren Hall*[4] where the defendant mounted the pavement on a bicycle and killed an elderly man. The defendant, after appeal, received seven months' immediate custody and a driving disqualification of 12 months. Although this decision was appealed, the Court of Appeal was of the view that, as the defendant was not sufficiently responsible to ride a bicycle, he ought not to drive a vehicle at all.

13.14   However, the court in *Hall* also held that penalty points could not be imposed because, in order for this to be done, the vehicle in question had to be mechanically propelled. Therefore, an offence concerning a bicycle does not provide the court with discretion to impose penalty points.

13.15   Under section 153 of the Sentencing Act 2020, the court also has the power to make a deprivation order in respect of the vehicle used to commit the offence.

4   [2009] EWCA Crim 2236.

Chapter 14

Dangerous driving causing serious injury

Caitlin Evans

14.1   The offence of causing serious injury by dangerous driving is set out in section 1A of the Road Traffic Act 1988 ('RTA 1988') which stipulates that, 'a person who causes serious injury to another person by driving a mechanically propelled vehicle dangerously on a road or other public place is guilty of an offence'.

ELEMENTS

Dangerous driving

14.2   Dangerous driving is covered in Chapter 12.

Causing

14.3   The prosecution must prove that the defendant caused the serious injury by driving dangerously.

14.4   The usual rules of causation apply. The dangerous driving does not need to be a substantial or major cause but simply more than 'de minimis'[1]. In *R v Kimsey*[2] the court approved of the trial judge's wording that the dangerous driving must be more than a 'slight or trifling' cause.

14.5   In *R v Barnes*[3], it was held that the jury must be sure the dangerous driving was an 'actual' cause of the accident in which the death (or injury)

---

1   *R v Hennigan* [1971] 3 All ER 133.
2   [1996] Crim LR 35.
3   [2008] EWCA Crim 2726, [2009] RTR 21.

occurred rather than one which 'creates the circumstances of a fatal collision'. However, on the facts of this case, the appeal against conviction was dismissed. The defendant and a friend were moving a sofa which had not been secured and, whilst in transit, it flew out of the back of the van. A motorcyclist avoided the sofa but, whilst attempting to warn motorists behind him, drove into the back of the defendant's van which was parked off the road, and died.

14.6   Guidance was given in *R v Girdler*[4] as to the liability of those involved in a first crash, when the fatality (or serious injury) occurred in a subsequent collision. The defendant's car collided with a taxi. The taxi was propelled into the fast lane of traffic. Despite many vehicles passing the taxi without further incident, a third vehicle collided with it. The driver of the third vehicle and the taxi driver both died. The court suggested that, to be liable for the fatality, the fatal incident should be a 'reasonably foreseeable' result of the dangerous driving. The jury should be directed that:

> 'the defendant will have caused the death(s) only if you are sure that it could sensibly have been anticipated that a fatal collision might occur in the circumstances in which the second collision did occur.'

14.7   In *R v Maybin*[5] and *R v Wallace (Berlinah)*[6], the court further clarified that the guidance in *Girdler* did not dictate that the jury must find that the exact circumstances of the fatal incident 'could sensibly have been anticipated' but rather look at the more general character of what had happened.

Serious injury

14.8   Serious injury is defined in section 1A(2) of the RTA 1988 as physical harm which amounts to grievous bodily harm for the purposes of the Offences Against the Person Act 1861.

DEFENCES

14.9   Defences are covered in detail in Chapter 16. The defences applicable to dangerous driving, such as automatism and duress of circumstances, are equally applicable to causing serious injury by dangerous driving.

14.10   No offence is committed where the driving took place in a public place other than a road during an authorised motoring event (RTA 1988, s 13A).

---

4   [2009] EWCA Crim 2666, [2010] RTR 28.
5   [2012] 2 SCR 30.
6   [2018] EWCA Crim 690.

ALLOCATION

14.11   The offence is triable either way.

ALTERNATIVE VERDICTS

14.12   Section 2 of the RTA 1988 (dangerous driving) and section 3 of the RTA 1988 (careless and inconsiderate driving) are available alternatives to this offence.

SENTENCING

14.13   The maximum sentence when tried summarily is six months' imprisonment, or an unlimited fine or both.

14.14   The maximum sentence on indictment is five years' imprisonment, or an unlimited fine, or both.

Sentencing Guidelines

14.15   At present, there are no sentencing guidelines for this offence but, as has been referred to in other chapters, this is likely to change, as causing serious injury by dangerous driving is one of the driving offences for which a consultation guideline is currently being considered by the Sentencing Council.

14.16   The current approach has been for the court to refer to the guidelines for causing death by dangerous driving. This was a course approved in *R v Dewdney*[7]. The sentencing judge should first consider the three levels of culpability found in those guidelines. There will then 'of necessity be a degree of compression in the sentences available to the court', as the maximum sentence for this offence is only five years' imprisonment, whereas causing death by dangerous driving carries a maximum of 14 years' imprisonment.

14.17   When using the guidelines, the court should consider that the 'consequences of the driving will be different and the standard of driving being considered may differ'[8].

---

7   [2014] EWCA Crim 1722.
8   *R v Ellis* [2014] EWCA Crim 593.

14.18   An example of where the guidelines have been used can be found in *R v Howsego*[9]. In that case, the defendant's driving constituted level three driving, meaning it created a 'significant' level of danger. He had driven at speed on the wrong side of the road, causing a head-on collision. However, the aggravating features (the defendant's previous convictions, driving a stolen vehicle, driving without insurance, and leaving the scene) meant that it was elevated into level two. The Court of Appeal stated that, after a trial and prior to any mitigation, the offence should have attracted a starting point of three and a half years. The Trial Judge's starting point of four years would have been more appropriate if it had been a level one case.

14.19   The causing death by dangerous driving guidelines are available on the Sentencing Council website[10].

ANCILLARY ORDERS

Disqualification

14.20   Under the Road Traffic Offenders Act 1988 ('RTOA 1988'), the offence carries an obligatory disqualification of two years unless special reasons are found (RTOA 1988, s 34(1) and (4)). If special reasons are found, the court has a discretion to impose less than the obligatory disqualification period or no disqualification at all.

14.21   Under section 35A of the RTOA 1988 and section 166 of the Sentencing Act 2020, the period of disqualification must be extended to cover the period for which the defendant will be in custody. In most cases, this will equate to an extension of half the custodial term passed.

14.22   Under section 35B of the RTOA 1988 and section 167 of the Sentencing Act 2020, if the court has imposed a custodial sentence for another offence, or where the defendant is already serving a custodial sentence, the court must consider the effect the longer period of incarceration will have on the disqualification. The court should 'so far as it is appropriate to do so' uplift the period of disqualification further so that the original period of disqualification (prior to the extension and possible uplift under sections 166 and 167) is served in full on release from prison.

---

9   [2016] EWCA Crim 120.
10   www.sentencingcouncil.org.uk/offences/crown-court/item/causing-death-by-dangerous-driving.

14.23 An order for disqualification until the offender passes an extended driving test is also mandatory under section 36 of the RTOA 1988.

Endorsement

14.24 The defendant's licence will be endorsed for four years from the date of the offence with the particulars of the conviction and the disqualification. However, if special reasons were found so that the defendant avoided disqualification, under section 44(1) of the RTOA 1988, the licence should be endorsed for four years with the particulars of the offence, and three to 11 penalty points. Under section 44(2) of the RTOA 1988, the court – if 'for special reasons it thinks fit not to do so' – need not even endorse the licence with the conviction and penalty points.

Deprivation

14.25 Under section 153 of the Sentencing Act 2020, the court may make a deprivation order in respect of the vehicle which was used to commit the offence if:

- it has been lawfully seized from the offender, or
- it was in the offender's possession or control when they were apprehended or when a summons in respect of the offence was issued.

POSTSCRIPT

14.26 A new offence of causing serious injury by careless driving came into force on 28 June 2022. This offence is the result of the Police, Crime and Sentencing Act 2022, which inserted section 2C into the RTA 1988. The elements of the offence are the same as that for causing serious injury by dangerous driving, with the obvious exception that the standard of driving need only satisfy the requirements for careless driving. Therefore, if the standard of driving falls below that of a careful and competent driver, and serious injury is caused, the offence is committed. It is triable either way and the maximum sentence, if convicted in the Crown Court, is two years' imprisonment. The offence also carries obligatory disqualification, unless the court finds special reasons.

Chapter 15

Causing death by dangerous driving or careless driving

Ray Tully KC

15.1   This chapter covers the following serious offences:

- causing death by dangerous driving – section 1 of the Road Traffic Act 1988 ('RTA 1998');

- causing death by careless or inconsiderate driving – section 2B of the RTA 1988; and

- causing death by careless or inconsiderate driving when under the influence – section 3A of the RTA 1988.

CAUSING DEATH BY DANGEROUS DRIVING (RTA 1988, s 1)

15.2   This offence is triable only on indictment and the maximum sentence is 14 years' imprisonment. However, for offences committed on or after 28 June 2022, the maximum sentence is life imprisonment. There is a minimum disqualification of two years, but this increases to five years for offences committed on or after 28 June 2022.

15.3   The statutory definition of 'dangerous driving' is contained in section 2A of the Road Traffic Act 1988 ('RTA 1988') and set out in detail within Chapter 12. The key elements of the offence involve consideration of what is essentially a two-limb test – it must be proven that:

- the driving which caused death 'falls far below' that which would be expected of the careful and competent driver; and

- it would be 'obvious' that the driving was such to a careful and competent driver.

Case preparation

15.4   There are some common features that apply equally to the different forms of fatal cases covered within this chapter.

Tone

15.5   The most important thing for any practitioner to bear in mind when dealing with such cases is that they represent a form of *homicide*. Someone has sadly died. That fact is inescapable and hangs over the entire court proceedings. Never, ever lose sight of that fact. From the outset, make sure you get your 'tone' right. Be alert to the sensitivities that arise for all involved in the case. For example, try to avoid the type of crass mistake made by this author, who turned up at court to deal with sentencing in a death by dangerous driving case carrying his robes in a lovely new bag recently given to him as a present but which was, unfortunately, emblazoned with images of speedometers from classic cars. That is not a good look. Thank goodness for the kindly security staff who pointed it out before any harm was done.

The parties

15.6   Getting the basics right, most importantly, includes learning the name of the deceased. It is all too easy to get it wrong or to forget it. The deceased is not a witness in the case (for obvious reasons). They are, however, the most important person in the whole case. Write down their name. Commit it to memory. Don't *ever* get it wrong.

15.7   The impact of the fatality applies on both sides of the case. When prosecuting, take time to understand the deceased's family dynamics. Make full use of the Family Liaison Officer ('FLO') in advance of and during any trial. In a world that increasingly involves 'blended' families, it may be necessary to meet separately with different members of the same family. If the case involves a marginal decision about whether it should be prosecuted as dangerous or careless (and many do), then explain the issues to the deceased's family in advance (assuming they are not witnesses of fact).

15.8   If defending, make sure the defendant and their family understand the there is only one *victim* involved in the case. It is sometimes possible for them to lose sight of that fact in the adversarial hurly-burly of a court setting. It may be necessary to forcefully insist they understand that fact and behave accordingly throughout the case.

15.9   Also take time to think about the physical arrangements inside the courtroom. Discuss them in advance with the usher and your opponent to ensure everyone knows what the plan is. It may involve micro-managing who is sitting where in court and in what order people arrive and depart the courtroom. These are small things, but they are important to the smooth running of the case. It means you are being courteous to all involved in what is likely to be a highly charged situation.

15.10   You may also notice that there are 'random' individuals who appear to be taking a keen interest in the case. Find out who they are. Most likely, they will be from an insurance company that has a vested interest in the outcome of the case. They frequently appoint an advocate to keep a 'Noting Brief' of the proceedings.

Law and facts

15.11   Get the law and the facts of the case straight in your head. It sounds basic and it is, but the facts can be confusing for all concerned, so make sure *you* master them.

15.12   Spend time understanding how the different factual accounts fit together into an overall narrative scheme. Make sure you understand the relative positioning of the vehicles involved as well as the positioning of all witnesses to the event (including any pedestrians). It can be a good idea to start this process by simply mapping out the relative positions and direction of travel of the vehicles involved on a clean sheet of paper.

15.13   Few types of case are as dependent upon the use of maps, plans and photographs, as those involving fatal collisions. Think about the presentation of the evidence well in advance of trial. If *you* don't fully understand how the various narrative accounts fit together by reference to the available exhibits, how can you expect the judge, jury or witnesses to have any chance of following the evidence?

15.14   Understand the road layout. If you have time, it is always worth visiting the scene, especially if it is unfamiliar to you. Failing that, the police will usually have carried out a 'drive through' and/or a 'walk through' of the scene. If they have not done this, you may wish to ask them to do so. Consider whether this is sufficient for your purposes. Will a jury site visit be required? They are quite rare these days but might be needed. If so, you will need to highlight this request at the Plea and Trial Preparation Hearing ('PTPH').

111

Experts

15.15 With the possible exception of 'baby-shaking' cases, few other criminal cases rely so heavily upon the use of expert evidence. The use of experts in road traffic cases generally is the subject of Chapter 17. I do not seek to replicate here the guidance set out in that chapter. However, I do wish to underline the importance of expert evidence in this type of case. It is likely that at least two types of expert will feature in most fatal cases – collision investigators and vehicle examiners.

Collision investigators

15.16 When prosecuting, the collision investigator in most cases will be a serving police officer who has acquired some specialist training. Make sure you have a conference with them at an early stage. Go through their report. Make sure you understand the rationale underpinning their conclusions. Don't be afraid to challenge them. You won't get through the trial process without that happening. Don't be afraid, either, to ask basic questions that may risk exposing your own lack of understanding about technical issues. There is every chance that members of the jury will not have sufficient expertise to understand technical matters without having them carefully explained.

15.17 Defence experts in this area are often retired police officers who were once collision investigators. To that extent they are 'gamekeepers turned poachers'. Ensure that they are properly instructed and understand what you believe to be the key issues in the case. Make sure your expert has seen *all* the relevant material required for forming their opinion. You may want to write out a series of questions or propositions that you wish them to address in their report. Try to arrange a conference with them when you have received their initial report. Again, don't be afraid to test the basis for any stated opinion, nor to ask what may appear to be basic questions about their reasoning.

15.18 It is likely that the court will have directed the experts on either side to liaise and prepare a joint position statement setting out heads of agreement and disagreement, in accordance with Part 19.6 of the Criminal Procedure Rules 2020.

Vehicle examiners

15.19 As part of the police investigation, the vehicles involved will have been examined to see whether they had any relevant mechanical defects; typically, these will relate to tyres or brakes. If any defect is identified, consider first whether it was in any way causative of the collision. If it was not causative, it may have no relevance and be inadmissible.

15.20 When considering issues relating to the state of the defendant's vehicle, it is also important to bear in mind the impact of section 2A(2) of the RTA 1988. Driving is considered to be dangerous per se 'if it would be obvious to a competent and careful driver that driving in that way would be dangerous'. The dangerous state of the vehicle needs to be such that it would be 'seen or realised at first glance'. This aspect is sometimes highly significant where the owner of a commercial vehicle is also charged. It is possible that the owner who is responsible for the upkeep of the vehicle is aware of maintenance issues unknown to the actual driver.

Other experts

15.21 It is sometimes possible that other types of expert may be instructed in a fatal collision case. If that is so, it is important to ensure they have a proper knowledge of the wider issues in the case that go beyond their own specialist field of expertise. One example that illustrates the importance of this approach concerned the instruction of a medical expert in a case involving the suggestion that a defendant lorry driver had 'blacked-out' momentarily before a fatal collision due to a latent heart condition. Unfortunately, the eminent cardiologist instructed had not been made fully aware of several eye-witness accounts regarding a course of driving over a 20-minute period leading up to the collision. The value of the expert's opinion in such circumstances was rendered practically worthless, with obvious consequences for the defendant's case.

Sentencing guidelines

15.22 The stakes are high in this type of case. If the case is assessed as Level 1 or Level 2, the defendant will certainly receive a lengthy prison sentence. Even if the case is assessed as being a Level 3 offence, prison is overwhelmingly the most likely outcome. It will be rare for any case to fall at the very bottom end of Level 3 and to open up the possibility of a suspended sentence (at least in theory).

15.23 This is obviously a very significant outcome in any circumstances, but it is in the nature of these cases that those involved are often individuals who have had no other interaction with the criminal justice system (and never will have in the future). Quite commonly, the defendant will be a person of good character, in good employment and from a loving family. The impact of a prison sentence is feared and keenly felt.

15.24 Paradoxically, in no other type of case is there regularly such a disparity between the sentencing expectations on the part of a deceased's family and the likely sentence that will be passed by the judge. These issues need to be carefully managed on both sides of the case.

15.25 When prosecuting, it is necessary and appropriate to ensure that the deceased's family is fully informed about the operation of the Sentencing Guidelines to the case. The guidelines are public documents and easily available online. They can and should be encouraged to consider them and ask any questions they may have about their application to the case.

15.26 Likewise, when defending, ensure that the defendant and their family are properly acquainted with application of the guidelines to the facts of the case.

15.27 One of the key issues that often arises in these types of case is the disparity in sentence resulting from whether the case falls within the guideline for death by dangerous driving or death by careless driving. There are significant differences between the two. There is more on that particular topic below.

CAUSING DEATH BY CARELESS OR INCONSIDERATE DRIVING (RTA 1988, S 2B)

15.28 This offence is triable either-way and the maximum sentence is five years' imprisonment. Disqualification is mandatory, and for a minimum of 12 months, unless the court finds that there are special reasons not to disqualify.

15.29 The statutory definition of 'careless driving' is contained in section 3ZA of the RTA 1988. It is considered in detail within Chapter 11.

15.30 The key elements of the offence involve consideration of whether the defendant can be proven to have caused death by (1) driving without 'due care and attention' – that is defined as driving which 'falls below what would be expected of a competent and careful driver', or (2) driving 'without reasonable consideration for others' – this limb requires proof that other people were inconvenienced by the driving.

15.31 This offence has developed over time. When this practitioner started out, the offence did not even exist! When it came into force, it was considered to be a somewhat controversial development. The maximum sentence was initially set at six months' imprisonment, before later being increased to five years.

15.32   All of the observations set out above regarding practical tips on how to conduct death by dangerous driving cases apply equally to cases involving death by careless driving (and, in some instances, even more so). This is certainly true with regards to 'tone', particularly when defending. There is a greater likelihood that a defendant may feel 'victimised' simply because of being prosecuted, as the driving in question may be less obviously culpable. At the bottom end of the scale for such offences, the decision to prosecute is often highly marginal and may have taken a long time to be decided upon. That can give rise to a sense of grievance on the part of a defendant that needs to be carefully managed.

15.33   It will be borne in mind that the prosecution does not have to prove that the alleged careless or inconsiderate driving was the sole, main or even a significant cause of the fatality – simply that it was *a* cause.

15.34   When prosecuting, it is important to ensure that the family of the deceased are properly aware of the issues in the case and the legal test. If it is a marginal case, their expectations will also need to be addressed. This should be done sensitively but honestly. They should be similarly advised when it comes to informing them of the likely sentence that will follow in the event of a plea or conviction after trial. They should be made fully aware of the Sentencing Council Guidelines and encouraged to fully acquaint themselves with it. They will then be better able to comprehend the proceedings and the eventual outcome.

15.35   When defending, there is greater scope for avoiding an immediate custodial sentence if convicted of this offence. The crucial factor will be the degree of culpability involved in the driving itself. Sentencing submissions should be tailored to reflect the relevant criteria set out in the Definitive Guideline.

15.36   Sometimes, the determining factor as to whether an immediate custodial sentence is merited in a mid-range or top-end death by careless case will be the plea itself. That can bring its own pressures, especially when dealing with those unfamiliar with the courts. It will be important to ensure that the defendant is not placed under undue pressure, but equally important that you are able to provide clear advice. It may be appropriate to consider whether a 'Goodyear indication' (a request from the defence that the judge indicate the maximum sentence before a plea is entered) would be of assistance to a defendant who is struggling to resolve their position. In all circumstances, ensure that you obtain fully signed instructions.

CAUSING DEATH BY CARELESS OR INCONSIDERATE DRIVING WHEN UNDER THE INFLUENCE (RTA 1988, s 3A)

15.37   This offence is triable only on indictment and the maximum sentence is 14 years' imprisonment. However, as with causing death by dangerous driving, for offences committed on or after 28 June 2022, the maximum sentence is life imprisonment. The minimum period of disqualification is also increased from two years to five years for offences committed on or after 28 June 2022.

15.38   The general comments set out above regarding death by dangerous cases apply to this offence as well.

15.39   The elements of the offence are the same as for causing death by careless / inconsiderate driving, but with the additional element that, at the time of driving, one of the aggravating features identified within section 3A(1) is present. Typically, this will involve driving with excess alcohol or where there is evidence regarding the presence of illegal drugs.

15.40   It will be noted that, so far as the presence of drugs is concerned, this is in effect a strict liability offence. It is not necessary that the presence of drugs render the driver 'unfit' or that they were in any way causative of the fatality.

15.41   For public policy reasons, a zero-tolerance approach is taken to the issue of driving with evidence of *any* illegal drugs in the system. This is in stark contrast to alcohol, where a certain level is tolerated by statute. Many drugs remain in the system for a significant period after they have been consumed. It may therefore come as something of a surprise for a defendant to learn that they were driving whilst 'over the limit', and to learn just how far over the limit they were. You may well find yourself representing someone who is two or three times over the legal limit and yet telling you they felt completely unaffected by the drugs they had consumed. Their perception of such matters is utterly irrelevant.

15.42   The net effect of this legislation is that a defendant who has consumed cannabis (perhaps days earlier), who then causes a fatality by driving carelessly, is subject to a maximum sentence of life imprisonment, rather than five years' imprisonment which would otherwise be the case. It clearly has the scope to make a considerable difference to the outcome.

15.43   That step-change in the sentencing regime is reflected in the Definitive Guideline covering this offence. Where drugs have been consumed, it will be almost impossible to avoid an immediate custodial sentence of some length. That is simply a fact of life, and any client will have to be advised accordingly.

Note

15.44   There is one further offence that might fall to be considered within this chapter, namely 'causing death by driving: unlicensed, disqualified or uninsured drivers'.

15.45   This is an offence under section 3ZB of the RTA 1988. In comparison to the other offences in this chapter, it is very rarely encountered in practice and so has not been covered.

Chapter 16

Defences

Peter Binder

> *'In cases of Defense 'tis best to weigh*
> *The Enemy more mighty than he seems.'*

16.1 Shakespeare's admonition from 'Henry V' never to underestimate one's opponent is a salutary reminder that in our jurisdiction we operate in an adversarial system, and that if one is to contest a driving offence, no matter what the level of seriousness, the usual rules of engagement apply, ie the burden of proving each aspect of the offence lies with the prosecution (unless the offence is one of those to which a statutory exception applies), and it is the role of the defence advocate to do all they can, within the rules of course, to prevent the prosecution from succeeding. One should always assume (although experience teaches that it is not *always* the case in practice) that the prosecution will be thoroughly prepared for trial, and it goes without saying that, if you are defending, you will be too. That process begins, however, with an analysis of the legal ingredients of the charge your client faces, together with an understanding of the defences that are available to them, both in legal as well as factual terms.

16.2 This chapter is not directed to the endless array of different factual circumstances that may provide a defence ('I didn't actually go through the lights on red', 'The officer's estimate of my speed was wrong', 'It wasn't me driving the vehicle' etc) but to a number of specific defences that can sometimes arise in the context of road traffic law. The examples given below are intended as an overview of the topic. The law and procedure concerning defences can be complicated, and it is always worth consulting the legislation and guideline cases themselves.

DRIVING WITH EXCESS ALCOHOL AND DRUG OFFENCES (RTA 1988, ss 4, 5 AND 5A)

16.3 A not-uncommon line of defence encountered in practice is where the driver's alcohol or drug level is said to be due to the consumption of alcohol or drugs subsequent to the time of the alleged offence (sometimes referred to as the 'hip-flask' defence). Post-offence consumption enables a defendant to argue that, were it not for alcohol consumed after the event, their ability to drive properly would not have been impaired (where the offence charged is under RTA 1988, s 4) or that the measurement of alcohol or drugs in the specimen provided subsequently to the police would have been less than the prescribed limit (where the offence is under RTA 1988, s 5 or 5A). The onus is always on the defendant to prove (on a balance of probabilities) that they consumed the quantity of alcohol or drugs in question after the time of driving or being in charge.

16.4   Unless it is obvious that the post-consumption explains the excess reading, the defence will have little, if any, prospect of success without the calling of scientific evidence demonstrating the effect of the post-consumption on the defendant's alcohol/drug levels. Accordingly, a suitably qualified expert invariably needs to be instructed in cases of this type. Similar considerations apply where a defendant wishes to argue that their drink has been 'spiked' for the purposes of a 'special reason' not to disqualify. It is important to bear in mind, however, that even if a defendant is able to provide scientific evidence in support of their case, they will still need to satisfy the court that their account of the post-consumption in question is credible.

16.5   It is also a defence for a motorist to show that the drug was provided for a medical reason (or by a dentist) and that the drug was taken in accordance with the directions given by the prescriber of the drug and by the manufacturer (see RTA 1988, s 5A(3)).

FAILING TO CO-OPERATE WITH A PRELIMINARY BREATH TEST (RTA 1988, s 6(6)) AND FAILING TO PROVIDE A SPECIMEN OF BLOOD, BREATH OR URINE (RTA 1988, s 7(6))

16.6   A motorist cannot be convicted of the section 6(6) offence if he has a reasonable excuse for failing to provide breath in the prescribed manner. If this defence is advanced, the burden shifts to the prosecution to disprove it. The case law establishes that a reasonable excuse can only arise where the motorist is physically or mentally unable to provide the specimen, or the provision of the specimen would entail a substantial risk to his health[1]. Physical issues such as bronchitis, asthma or lung disease might satisfy this requirement, depending upon the nature and degree of the condition involved. It could also be argued, depending again on the actual factual circumstances, that a failure to

1   *R v Lennard* [1973] RTR 252.

understand the requirement to co-operate with a preliminary test (for example, due to a motorist's limited understanding of English) amounted to a reasonable excuse on the basis the motorist was mentally unable to provide the specimen. Physical or mental inability due to reasons that are self-induced (for example, due to the voluntary consumption of alcohol) would, however, not be considered 'reasonable'[2].

16.7   The section 7(6) offence is also only committed where the motorist has no reasonable excuse for the failure, due to their physical and mental inability, to comply with the requirement to provide the specimen in question. By way of example, it has been held that a phobia of needles is capable of being a reasonable excuse for not providing a blood sample[3], but this will only succeed in practice where there is medical evidence in support. For a useful analysis of the law in this area, see *Martiner v DPP*[4].

DURESS AND NECESSITY

16.8   The defence of duress applies to road traffic offences as it does in the context of the criminal law more generally. It is for the defendant to raise the issue and for the prosecution to disprove it. In general terms, the defendant has to show that:

(i)   they reasonably believed they were threatened;

(ii)   they or a family member or someone for whom they felt responsible would be subject to almost immediate death or serious injury, and there was no reasonable way for the defendant to avoid the threat;

(iii)   the threat was the direct cause of the defendant committing the offence; and

(iv)   a sober person of reasonable firmness of the defendant's age, sex and character would have been driven to act as the defendant did.

16.9   The defence has been held to apply in cases of reckless driving[5] as well as on a charge of driving with excess alcohol[6], although it is important to be aware of the limits to the defence, in particular the fact the duress must be operative throughout the duration of the driving concerned[7].

---

2   *DPP v Beech* [1992] RTR 239.
3   *R v Harding* [1974] RTR 325.
4   [2004] EWHC 2484 (Admin).
5   *R v Willer* [1987] RTR 22.
6   *DPP v Bell* [1992] RTR 335.
7   *CPS v Brown* [2007] EWHC 3274 (Admin).

16.10   Necessity (sometimes referred to as 'duress of circumstances') has long been recognised as a defence in English law. In *R v Martin*[8], where the defendant had claimed that he was compelled to drive while disqualified in order to prevent his wife from committing suicide, it was said that the defence could arise from objective dangers threatening an accused or others and was available only where an accused could be said to have acted both reasonably and proportionately in order to avoid a threat of death or serious injury. In essence, it is governed by the same principles as those that apply to the more general (and more commonly used) defence of duress.

NON-INSANE AUTOMATISM

16.11   It is not uncommon for the question of 'automatism' to arise in driving cases. In brief terms, the defence involves an involuntary action or actions on the part of the accused, which are involuntary as a result of a failure of the mind not due to disease (if the failure was due to disease, the question of insanity would arise). It is, once again, an issue for the defendant to raise and for the prosecution to disprove. There is a chain of authorities, set out in the leading textbooks, which the advocate needs to be familiar with in order to run such a defence. The leading case is *R v Quick*[9], in which it was said that the defence was directed to the 'malfunctioning of the mind of transitory effect caused by the application to the body of some external factor such as violence, drugs, including anaesthetics, alcohol and hypnotic influences' (provided that it is not self-induced). This gives some idea of the general nature of the defence. It has been held to apply in road traffic cases where the accused driver has suffered a total loss of control due to unforeseen medical issues, such as an epileptic fit or a hypoglycaemic attack. Expert medical evidence will inevitably be required to establish a defence of automatism. Nevertheless, once the defence is established, the accused will escape liability provided that they were not at fault in inducing or failing to avoid the loss of control.

16.12   Automatism can also arise from external physical factors such as the accused being struck by a stone thrown up from the road surface or being attacked by a swarm of bees: see *Hill v Baxter*[10]. Conversely, a bus driver who claimed to have lost control of his vehicle, as a result of attempting to wave away a wasp, was found to have no defence to a charge of causing death by dangerous driving: see *R v Moses*[11]. In that case, the Court of Appeal agreed with the Crown's argument that the driver should have stopped the bus and then got rid of the wasp, and, as a result, upheld the conviction – which, for the convicted appellant, must have been a real sting in the tail …

8   [1989] RTR 63.
9   57 Cr App R 722.
10   [1958] 2 WLR 76.
11   [2004] EWCA Crim 2506.

Part 4

Experts

Chapter 17

Expert reports

Emily Evans

17.1   There is a superficial simplicity to road traffic offences, which can ultimately turn out to be some of the most technically difficult for practitioners to deal with. Crown Court advocates are rarely instructed in the summary-only offences which remain in the magistrates' court, such as drink or drug driving. Equally, those who practise regularly in the magistrates' court may not have much experience of these types of case because they frequently fail to pass the interests of justice test for legal aid. Nevertheless, any case which is likely to involve expert evidence will benefit significantly from having proper legal representation.

17.2   It is widely known amongst the legal fraternity that there are 'specialist road traffic defence' firms out there who will take advantage of defendants who have the means to pay privately to be represented. Their tactics are to request all of the material that the prosecution hold and to instruct experts on issues which, by the time the case comes to trial, fall away. These firms sometimes offer unrealistic advice to their clients, and it is only when an independent advocate is able to provide objective and reasoned advice on the day of trial that the client realises they have nowhere else to go and must plead guilty. This is little comfort to a defendant who, by this time, has accrued significant legal costs in addition to the cost of seeking expert reports which can run into the thousands.

17.3   As a defence advocate you are an officer of the court. Whilst it is your duty to represent the best interests of your client, you also have a concurrent – and primary – duty to the court and this includes the duty not to mislead the court. The first thing you must do upon receiving instructions is to identify the issues in the case. Once you have determined the relevant issues, you can then turn your mind to whether or not an expert report will be required. Expert reports are not required in every case, and an expert should only be instructed if their opinion has the potential to make a significant difference to the outcome.

TYPES OF EXPERT REPORT

17.4   There are many different types of expert in this field. The expertise required will depend upon the type of offence that the defendant is charged with and the nature of their defence. Whilst this book cannot seek to cover all scenarios that may crop up, the most common types of expert report are as follows:

- Speed calculations: in speeding offences where the speed recorded is disputed.

- Back-calculations: this arises in circumstances where a defendant claims that they consumed alcohol after driving (the 'hip-flask defence').

- Medical experts: this can arise in a number of different types of case. Such experts are most frequently encountered in cases involving a failure to provide, where the defendant claims that there was a good medical reason as to why they could not provide a specimen, or in cases where an automatism defence is being pursued.

- Psychiatric reports: these overlap with medical reports and will need to be sought in cases of failing to provide a sample where it is claimed that there is a psychiatric condition, such as a phobia of needles.

- Drug expert reports: these may be required in cases of drug driving to analyse the breakdown of drugs in the system and the time at which they were ingested.

- Collision scene investigation (see Chapter 15): these reports are sought in a range of different types of case but are especially important in driving incidents which resulted in a fatality. This type of expert report will provide conclusions as to how a collision occurred and who was at fault.

- Tachograph reports: tachographs record the speed and distance driven, so can be very useful in presenting evidence to show a course of driving.

- Mechanical expert reports: these reports will establish whether there were any mechanical faults, issues with the vehicle loading, and other aspects of the vehicle itself which can assist in establishing the cause of a collision. They may also assist with mitigation or highlighting whether a defence might be available.

- Post mortem and toxicology reports: a post mortem is required in any fatality case. This will establish the cause of death. A toxicology report will indicate whether there were any drugs in the system of an individual involved in a collision.

- Mobile phone experts: they will be able to establish whether a defendant was using his mobile phone at the time of driving and, potentially, whether it was a contributory factor to the incident.

- Cell site experts: this is something referred to later in this chapter. Cell site experts analyse the locations of mobile phones at particular times, which can assist in identifying who was driving a specific vehicle.

17.5 A recent case highlights the value of expert reports. The defendant was charged with dangerous driving and driving whilst unfit through drugs. The defendant had been travelling at excessive speed and had collided with a number of stationary vehicles at traffic lights. The defendant suffered serious and life-threatening injuries. He had to be treated at the scene and was hospitalised for many months. There were a number of eyewitnesses to the collision, but all that could be said was that the defendant was out of control and travelling at a significant speed. The defendant had no recollection of the event due to the injuries he sustained. He suffered with epilepsy and believed that he had experienced an epileptic fit at the wheel. The toxicology report showed that the defendant had ketamine in his blood. However, the medical expert report commissioned by the defence revealed that, rather than being the result of recreational drug use, the ketamine had in fact been administered by paramedics at the roadside when treating the defendant.

FUNDING

17.6 If a defendant is privately paying, the solicitor should identify a handful of experts who can provide quotes, taking into account the nature of the work required and the number of hours it will take them to complete a report. You should bear in mind that there will be an additional cost for the expert to attend trial, and those costs should also be communicated to the client in writing.

17.7 If the client is legally aided, prior authority will need to be sought from the Legal Aid Authority. They will require a CRM4 form to be completed on the electronic system. You will need the expert to set out their estimated hours of preparation and travel, as well as the relevant hourly rate. You will usually have to show that you have obtained at least two quotes and opt for the lesser of the two, given that the funds will be paid from the public purse.

HOW TO OBTAIN AN EXPERT REPORT

17.8 To obtain an initial quote from any expert, you are usually required to provide them with the relevant prosecution evidence. Typically, this takes the form of the Initial Disclosure of the Prosecution Case but it can also include supplementary statements and even expert reports served by the prosecution. It is always helpful to set out in a letter of instruction to the expert what the defendant's instructions are and the relevant issues in the case. You will then need to outline the issues that you would like the expert to look at and the specific questions that require an expert opinion.

SERVICE OF EXPERT REPORTS

17.9 Once you are in receipt of the report, it is important that you read it and understand it as soon as you can. If there are areas that require clarification, it is useful to telephone the expert directly and ask them to explain it to you or to clarify the point in writing. Sometimes, experts set out their findings and conclusions in language which they are familiar with, but others are not. This can cause confusion or misunderstanding. It is particularly important that you are able to explain the expert's findings to your lay client, so it is imperative that you understand what the expert is saying.

17.10 Occasionally, you may be presented with an expert report which undermines your client's defence and/or adds weight to the prosecution case. In these circumstances, it is important that you explain this carefully to your client and you should advise your client that it is not in his best interests to serve or rely upon that report.

17.11 An example of such a judgement call in respect of a defence expert report arose in a case in which the prosecution provided a witness statement from an analyst who produced a number of maps showing cell site data and Automatic Number Plate Recognition (ANPR) data. This type of data is common in road traffic cases where the driver cannot be identified. Cell site evidence can be used to establish where a particular mobile phone is located during a period of time. ANPR cameras are located on roads all over the country, so are used to indicate where a specific car is at a specific time. Where this combined evidence establishes that a mobile phone is moving in tandem with a car, it can be inferred that the user of the phone is driving the car. The prosecution had failed to instruct their expert to deal with the interpretation and limitations of the cell site data. Conversely, the defence did instruct an expert to analyse the data and provide an interpretation to assist with the issues in the case. The defence expert's conclusions were unsupportive of the defence case and, as a result, the defence did not serve that report or rely on it at trial. Instead, the defence made a section 78 application to exclude the cell site data presented by the prosecution analyst on the basis that no expert had been instructed by the prosecution to properly explain that evidence to the court.

17.12 If, however, the expert report is favourable to the defendant, it must be served upon the prosecution in accordance with Rule 19 of the Criminal Procedure Rules 2020. The expert will also need to be familiar with Rule 19, as it sets out their obligations and their duty to the court. The prosecution will then consider whether they wish to instruct their own expert, or instruct their existing expert to provide a further report in response to the defence report. If they wish to rely upon any such expert report, they will need to serve it upon the defence. The court may then invite the two respective experts to meet and identify points of agreement and points of dispute. This is intended to reduce the need for lengthy and complicated expert evidence and to clarify the issues that the tribunal of fact needs to concentrate upon. Both experts will need to be warned to attend the trial in order to give oral evidence.

HOW TO HANDLE EXPERT WITNESSES AT TRIAL

17.13   Expert witnesses are treated very differently to civilian witnesses at trial. Civilian witnesses are usually taken to the witness suite and kept apart from the defendant and defence witnesses. The same cannot be said of expert witnesses. It is common practice for the opposing experts to meet prior to the hearing and discuss any issues that may have arisen. As outlined above, it is expected that they will have reached areas of agreement and disagreement, but they may wish to discuss these further at court. It is common for experts to be asked to consider specific questions during the course of the trial or hearing, and they can continue their discussions even once the trial is underway. Sometimes, experts are asked to draw up a schedule of the areas of agreement and disagreement to clarify the points in dispute.

17.14   The experts should give evidence back-to-back. The defence expert will therefore be called out of turn and give their evidence immediately after the prosecution expert. This is to enable the expert evidence to be considered together.

Part 5

Sentencing

Chapter 18

Opening a case for sentence

Alistair Haggerty

18.1   When opening a case for sentence, your role as prosecutor is to present the facts fairly, clearly and comprehensively. Whilst your counterpart acting for the defence will endeavour to achieve the lowest sentence possible for their client, it is inappropriate for a prosecutor to counteract this by arguing for a higher sentence. Whilst there may be a temptation to emphasise the worst aspects of the defendant's conduct, this should be avoided. The prosecutor is an officer of the court and has a duty to be neutral with regard to sentence.

18.2   This duty does not mean that opening a case for sentence is straightforward. As with other aspects of advocacy, preparation is key. When you are instructed to prosecute a sentence in a driving case, you should check that you have the following as soon as possible:

(i)   A police summary of the facts of the case (often referred to as the MG5).

(ii)   The witness statements.

(iii)   The victim personal statement(s). You will also need to check whether the victim would like the statement read aloud in court.

(iv)   The exhibits.

(v)   Access to any relevant CCTV, dash camera, or police body camera footage. This will most likely be referred to in the case summary but can often be overlooked when the papers are provided to counsel. It is sometimes the most important evidence in the case and the judge or magistrates' bench will want to view it before deciding the sentence. It will need to be played at the hearing, so check that it is available in a format which is compatible with your computer and can be played in court.

(vi)   The defendant's previous convictions (the PNC print).

(vii)   A copy of the defendant's Driver Record Enquiry Report (driving record)[1]. It is standard practice for a list of the defendant's previous

---

1   See Chapter 2, which covers this in detail.

convictions to be included in the papers, but the driving record – typically in the form of a print from the DVLA – is generally not obtained as a matter of course. Nevertheless, aside from cases in which a lengthy disqualification is automatic, the judge or bench will want to know something about the defendant's driving record. Do they have a history of accumulating penalty points? Have they previously been disqualified as a totter (disqualifications following a criminal conviction should be recorded on the PNC print)? How many points do they currently have on their licence? You will need to be well-placed to answer these questions, so make a request for the defendant's driving record print.

(viii) Details of whether compensation ought to be applied for and, if so, how much. Compensation in driving cases is sometimes covered by the insurers, but an enquiry should be made with those instructing you to check whether an application will need to be made at the hearing. The police should have a record of the losses incurred by the injured party (such as the cost of medical treatment and financial loss due to being unable to work), which you will need to have access to in order to justify the amount of compensation applied for.

18.3   If you are fortunate enough to be briefed well in advance of the sentencing hearing, you will be able to identify the further information required at an early stage. However, you might not be instructed until the afternoon before the hearing. If you are in this position, and you discover that important material is missing, speak to those instructing you as soon as you can. You will be surprised at how quickly material can be sent to you when it is urgently needed for a sentencing hearing. Even if important evidence, such as video footage, is supplied just before the hearing is about to be called on, do not be afraid to ask the judge for a few minutes to view it and ensure that it can be played in court. Only a very impatient judge would refuse such a request, and most will be grateful for having the material properly presented before the court.

18.4   Maps can be especially useful in driving cases. They provide the judge with an idea of the distance driven, the nature of the roads, and the relevant features and hazards. If a map has not been served with the papers, but you think it would be useful, ask the police to provide one. If this cannot be done before the hearing, take a screenshot from an online map. Provided you show this to your opponent before the hearing, there will generally be no objection to it being adduced as part of your opening.

18.5   Having checked that you have all the material, the next stage is to prepare the structure of your submissions. When opening a case for sentence, there are generally four parts:

(i)   The facts, including, if appropriate, reference to the stage at which guilty pleas were entered.

(ii)   The defendant's antecedents and driving record.

(iii) The sentencing guidelines.

(iv)   Ancillary orders.

THE FACTS

18.6   The golden rule, when opening the facts for sentence, is to not simply read from the police summary. It can be a useful aide-memoire and will provide you with an overview of the case, but it may well be inaccurate. This is because it is written at an early stage of the case, which can render it incomplete or aspirational – setting out how it is anticipated that the evidence will emerge, rather than properly reflecting the way in which the evidence has emerged. Instead of relying on the police summary, write your own by reviewing the witness statements and extracting the most salient evidence. It can be impactive to quote directly from witness statements, but do this sparingly. The recital of the facts should be in your own words.

18.7   Your factual summary should be focused and relevant. In cases involving protracted dangerous driving, the narrative in witness statements can often read like a list of road names. Rather than going through these in your opening, highlight the aspects of the driving which made it dangerous, such as the number of traffic controlling measures which were ignored, the number of cars which had to take evasive action, and the damage done as a result of the defendant's actions. Similarly, when playing video footage, you only need to show the judge the relevant sections. You should be prepared to offer some narration to the footage and pick out important details.

18.8   Victim personal statements are generally read at the conclusion of the facts. Prior to the hearing, you should review the victim personal statement and identify any passages which should not be read out in court, particularly where the witness implores the judge to impose a lengthy prison sentence. Sometimes, the author of the statement indicates a preference for it not to be read aloud. In such situations, it is appropriate to draw the judge's attention to the statement and ensure that they have a copy. Occasionally, the witness will attend court to read the statement aloud themselves. When this happens, you should meet with the witness before the case is called on, to check whether they require any special measures. You might also need to explain to them that there are certain passages which should not be read. In most cases, the victim personal statement will be read by the prosecuting advocate.

THE DEFENDANT'S ANTECEDENTS AND DRIVING RECORD

18.9   Once you have dealt with the facts, it is usual to turn to the defendant's previous convictions and driving record. It is especially important to review the list of antecedents, to ascertain whether the most recent offence was committed during the currency of a suspended sentence, community order or conditional discharge. Equally, if the defendant was on licence at the time of the offence for which they are to be sentenced, this is an important aggravating feature. If the defendant has committed similar offences in the past, the judge might want to know a bit about their facts (for example, whether a previous conviction for dangerous driving was committed in similar circumstances to the present offence). Be prepared for this by identifying any similar previous offences and requesting a summary of their facts in advance of the hearing. Minimum periods of disqualification in driving cases can often be dictated by previous convictions and their dates, so be sure to check the relevant provisions before the hearing.

18.10   Be prepared to address the judge with regard to the defendant's driving record. As referred to above, in order to do this you are likely to need a document from the DVLA (which can be requested via the CPS and, sometimes, through the court clerk). It will be this, and not the PNC print, which will indicate whether the defendant is at risk of disqualification due to the accumulation of penalty points for speeding. It will also reveal whether the defendant is a persistent driving offender and whether they have previously been disqualified as a totter.

SENTENCING GUIDELINES

18.11   The judge will then require guidance regarding the sentencing guidelines. For cases in the magistrates' court, the relevant guidelines can be found on the Sentencing Council website. It is important to look at these, and the provisions governing penalty points and disqualification, prior to the hearing. However, these guidelines are not applicable in the Crown Court. At the time of writing, some offences, including dangerous driving and causing serious injury by dangerous or careless driving, do not have guidelines for use in the higher court. This is likely to change in the next year, as a consultation guideline, which includes these offences, is being considered by the Sentencing Council. Their review is likely to conclude in the autumn of 2022 and may well result in the publication of new guidelines. Until then, the current guideline on causing death by dangerous driving provides some assistance, especially in cases concerning serious injury, on the stepped approach to be followed by the judge. It can also be useful to look at sentencing cases considered by the Court of Appeal. Although many of these are fact-specific, some provide general principles to be considered by the court, and you may find a case which is factually very similar to the one you are prosecuting.

ANCILLARY ORDERS

18.12 The final matter to deal with, when opening a case for sentence, is ancillary orders. In addition to the usual orders which the court can make, such as costs and compensation, almost all driving offences result in the imposition of penalty points or disqualification from driving. You should be aware of the minimum and maximum penalties which the court can impose, and the suggested range in the sentencing guidelines. Where an offender has been recently convicted for a similar offence, the minimum period of disqualification is sometimes increased, so be sure to check this prior to the hearing. Some offences, such as dangerous driving, require the offender to undertake an extended retest before their licence can be renewed. Crown Court judges may not be familiar with the provisions governing penalty points and disqualification in driving cases because it is not their usual fare. You will quickly make a good impression if you have these details at your fingertips.

18.13 The court also has the power, under section 153 of the Sentencing Act 2020, to make a deprivation order in respect of the vehicle which was used to commit the offence. This is discussed in Chapter 14. If it appears to you that such an order may be appropriate, you should obtain instructions from the CPS as to whether they would like you to make the application.

18.14 Driving offences often attract publicity in the local and national press. This is partly because they resonate with a wide cross-section of the public – most adults have some experience of driving a car – but also because they can occasionally end in tragedy. If there is a journalist present, be aware that anything said in open court can be reported (subject to the reporting restrictions which can arise in very limited circumstances), so be mindful of the need to open the case sensitively and with a careful attention to detail.

Chapter 19

Mitigation

Peter Binder

19.1   The practical approach to be taken in seeking to mitigate (the lawyer's term) or lessen (the lay person's) the sentence imposed by a court for any road traffic offence will, of course, need to be tailored to both the nature of the offence (or, where there is more than one offence, the offences in combination with one another) and the unique, fact-specific, features of each individual case and each defendant. For serious road traffic offences, a defendant is very likely to be at considerable risk of a custodial sentence (in some instances, of many years' duration) while, at the other end of the spectrum, the court's sentencing powers are extremely limited and are confined to matters such as the number of penalty points to be imposed, the scale of any fine, and whether a period of disqualification is appropriate.

19.2   As such, the topic of 'Mitigation' covers a very broad canvas. The text that follows aims to set out some general principles before then demonstrating how they may apply in practice, by way of an example in the context of a case concerning causing death by dangerous driving. Some detail, of practical application, from an actual causing death by dangerous driving case then follows. It is hoped that this approach will be instructive, both to the practitioner and the lay person, whatever the nature of the case in which one is called upon to 'mitigate' sentence.

19.3   For the most serious offences, which are dealt with in the Crown Court, and particularly those involving a fatality such as causing death by dangerous or careless driving, a defendant will need to have specialist legal representation, invariably from a suitably qualified solicitor in the first instance. Once instructed, the solicitor will need to consider the approach to be taken with regard to mitigation at the earliest stage of the proceedings. The same applies to those cases involving what lawyers refer to as 'either-way' offences, which are those which can be dealt with either in the Crown Court or in the magistrates' court, depending upon the individual facts of the case and its seriousness. For this middle range of cases, a defendant should also take appropriate legal advice at the earliest possible stage. Where the offences are at the lower end of the spectrum and are triable only in the magistrates' court, defendants not infrequently choose to represent themselves, usually for financial reasons.

19.4 For the majority of road traffic offences, there are now sentencing guidelines in place, regularly updated by the Sentencing Council and easily accessible online, and all courts are required to follow the relevant guidelines unless the court is satisfied that it would be contrary to the interests of justice to do so (which is extremely rare in practice). Separate guidelines apply to the sentencing of defendants under the age of 18, those with mental health issues or neurological impairments, and those in breach of existing court orders. For offences for which there is no offence-specific sentencing guideline, a court must have regard to the 'General Guideline: Overarching Principles'.

19.5 Understandably, for the more serious offences, the sentencing exercise is likely to be more considered and more complex and, accordingly, the relevant guidelines can be extremely detailed. In a case of causing death by dangerous driving, for example, having identified the appropriate starting point for sentence, and having then considered those features of the case that aggravate the position, the court must consider mitigating factors.

19.6 Mitigating factors generally fall into two categories: those which relate to the offence, and those which concern the offender. There are a number of mitigating factors which are listed in the sentencing guidelines, but the list is not exhaustive. Any factors which are capable of reducing the seriousness of the offence, or have the potential to enable the court to see the offender in a more positive light, may be taken into account. The factors which are especially relevant to road traffic offences include whether or not the defendant has an exemplary driving record, whether he gave assistance at the scene, and whether or not there is evidence of genuine remorse on the defendant's part. Further mitigating factors specifically referred to in the guidelines include mental illness or disability, youth or age (where impacting on the defendant's level of responsibility), lack of driving experience (where a contributory factor) and features such as whether the defendant was seriously injured, whether the victim was a close friend or relative, and whether the driving concerned was in response to a genuine emergency.

19.7 It is usual, certainly in the more serious cases such as those involving a fatality, that prosecuting counsel provides a sentencing note to the court in advance of the actual sentencing hearing. Good practice requires something similar from the defence advocate in response. This makes good sense: the sentencing judge will inevitably take on board the prosecution case as articulated in prosecuting counsel's note prior to the hearing. Not only is this unlikely to contain much by way of mitigation, it will almost inevitably emphasise the aggravating features of the case. It is in the client's interests to redress that balance by providing a note of their own setting out in detail such mitigation as is available, as well as addressing questions such as where, within the sentencing guideline, the case ought to fall.

19.8 It is also good practice to provide a copy of the defence note to prosecution counsel, inviting them to indicate any areas of disagreement. The aim should be to agree the issues relevant to sentence in advance of the hearing itself and, if that is not possible, at least to have the opportunity of preparing in advance the arguments which will need to be made in relation to those issues that remain contentious.

19.9 What follows below is an example of a defence sentencing note provided on behalf of a defendant in a past case of causing death by dangerous driving, but amended to some extent in order to protect the identities of those involved. An acknowledgment of the very sad nature of such cases and the level of harm involved is often no bad thing, as per the first paragraph.

i. This is a particularly tragic case and nothing set out below is intended in any way to minimise or detract from the level of grief felt by those closest to the victim and articulated so movingly in the victim personal statements provided to the Court by members of the deceased's family.

ii. D does not take issue with the facts of the case, as set out in the Collision Investigator's report. In essence therefore, he falls to be sentenced for driving at excessive speed in poor weather and road conditions, ultimately resulting in the death of another road user.

iii. The Court has been provided in advance of this hearing with a number of character references and medical reports concerning D. The references speak with one voice of an accomplished, highly respected and much-loved individual who, this incident apart, has been a force for good in others' lives, but who now bears a very heavy personal burden as a consequence of the events giving rise to these proceedings. The medical reports confirm the impact of these proceedings on his mental health.

iv. Submissions on the application of the Sentencing Guideline.

a. This is on any reasonable view a Level 3 case where the risk of danger to other road users was characterized by D's failure to adjust his speed to a level that was appropriate for the prevailing conditions. A 'standard' Level 3 case provides for a starting point of 3 years and a range of 2-5 years, but the Court's attention is respectfully drawn to the specific guidance attached to this Level to the effect that, *'Where the driving is markedly less culpable than for this level, reference should be made to the starting point and range for the most serious level of causing death by careless driving'.*

b.   It is submitted that this is indeed a case that sits within the 'markedly less culpable' category due to the combination of factors present here, not least the unanticipated weather conditions, the relatively short duration of the dangerous driving involved, and the absence of any other aspects of D's driving characteristic of dangerous driving. The starting point for the more serious level of careless driving ('falling not far short of dangerous driving') is 15 months.

c.   The defence make the following submissions in relation to the 'determinants of seriousness' specified in the guideline:

- Awareness of risk – example given in the guideline: 'a prolonged, persistent and deliberate case of a very bad driving' – Clearly not the case here, the driving in question lasting for no more than a few seconds;

- Effect of alcohol or drugs – Not applicable here;

- Inappropriate speed of vehicle – examples given include greatly excessive speed, racing, competitive driving etc., as well as 'driving above the speed limit' or 'at a speed that is inappropriate for the prevailing road or weather conditions' – It is accepted that D's driving fell within the less serious categories described here;

- Seriously culpable behaviour of offender e.g. aggressive driving, driving while using handheld mobile phone, driving while attention avoidably distracted, driving when knowingly suffering from medical or physical condition, driving when knowingly deprived of adequate sleep or rest, driving poorly maintained vehicle – None applicable here;

- In terms of the victim, failing to have proper regard to vulnerable road users – Not the case here.

v.   Insofar as factors that mitigate D's position and therefore ought to result in the 'starting point' being adjusted downwards in D's favour, the Court will have regard not only to D's previous good driving record and the fact that he immediately went to the assistance of the deceased, summoned help and remained at the scene in order to assist with the investigation, but also to the significant level of remorse he has demonstrated and the very considerable impact the events in question have had on his mental health, as evidenced in the numerous letters of support from family, friends and colleagues which have been provided to the Court.

vi. Additional to those matters set out above, D is entitled to the appropriate level of credit for his timely plea of guilty.

vii. The Court will be well aware that while sentences of immediate custody are considered 'the norm' for offences of this type, it does not follow that they are inevitable, and the Guideline itself emphasizes that fact by setting out in full the approach the Court should take to the imposition of a custodial sentence, including consideration of both a community order and a suspended sentence as alternatives to immediate custody. In this case, it can properly be said that:

   a. There is nothing to suggest that this incident was anything other than a tragic 'one-off' event and that as such D does not present a continued risk or danger to the public. He will of course now be disqualified from driving for an appropriate period in any event;

   b. The effect of this tragedy on his mental health has of itself been very significant punishment and as such it would be wrong to conclude that only immediate custody can provide sufficient punishment; if anything, it would further compound his already fragile and vulnerable state, and to a disproportionate extent;

   c. There is no history of failing to comply with Court orders;

   d. The pre-sentence report confirms that there is in D's case a 'realistic prospect of rehabilitation';

   e. D's personal mitigation is exceptionally strong.

viii. In all the circumstances, it is respectfully submitted that the appropriate sentence in this particular case is one that does not result in immediate custody.

PRE-SENTENCE REPORTS

19.10 In many of the more serious cases, the court will have ordered a report from a probation officer prior to sentencing the defendant. It is again good practice to provide the author of the report with a copy of the defence sentencing note, so that they have more than just the prosecution case papers on which to base their understanding of the facts of the case. In anything other than the relatively straightforward type of case, this is something best not simply left to the defendant to articulate in their, often quite brief, interview with the report author. This sort of assistance from the defence representative can prove to be invaluable in obtaining a positive report from a probation officer who, without being able to consider both sides of the story, is less well-placed to properly comment, particularly on the more nuanced cases.

19.11   The author of the report should also be alerted to personal issues relevant to one's client, be they of a domestic nature or concerning, for example, their physical or mental health. Again, it is not always safe to assume that the defendant will mention everything of relevance in their probation interview. It is often useful to ensure that the report's author is provided, in advance of their meeting with the defendant, with medical records and other documents, such as character references, upon which the defence are relying.

19.12   As any experienced advocate knows, there is considerable benefit to be gained from a detailed, well-reasoned pre-sentence report containing alternative proposals to immediate custody. Anything that the defence representatives can do to enhance the likelihood of such a proposal amounts to time and effort well spent.

19.13   Not all road traffic cases are as serious as those referred to above. There are also sentencing guidelines at the other end of the spectrum, which understandably tend to be less detailed than those for the more serious offences. For speeding offences, for example, while acknowledging that the list of mitigating factors given is non-exhaustive, the guideline only refers to the defendant's driving record (where clean, or comparatively so), their previous character, and whether there was a 'genuine emergency established', with assistance to the prosecution and credit for a plea of guilty also mentioned. Even those cases, of course, merit consideration of the more general sentencing matters set out above.

19.14   It is to be noted that the Sentencing Council announced (on 7 July 2022) a three-month consultation period for a raft of new and revised guidelines for the more serious road traffic offences[1]. It seems relatively certain, therefore, that comprehensive new guidelines for such offences will be coming into force very shortly. It is incumbent on the practitioner in this area to keep abreast of such developments.

---

1   www.sentencingcouncil.org.uk/news/item/motoring-offences-proposed-sentencing-guidelines-published.

Chapter 20

Special reasons, mitigating circumstances and exceptional hardship

Peter Binder

INTRODUCTION

20.1   This chapter covers the ways in which the court can depart from what are otherwise highly prescriptive provisions governing penalty points and disqualification. Even the most minor of driving offences can put a driving licence in jeopardy, especially if the offender has already accumulated a number of penalty points. It is often the case that a well-presented special reasons or exceptional hardship argument can be the difference between retaining a driving licence and being disqualified.

20.2   'Special reasons' are those which enable a court to refrain from disqualifying a driver, or from endorsing their licence, for an offence where disqualification or endorsement is ordinarily obligatory. They often arise in cases which effectively involve strict liability, such as driving without insurance or drink driving.

20.3   Distinct from 'special reasons' are 'mitigating circumstances', which a court may use as grounds for not disqualifying, or for disqualifying for a shorter period, when considering a penalty points disqualification. These situations tend to arise in circumstances where imposing the prescribed number of points in the legislation would result in the offender being disqualified for a period of at least six months (and, in certain circumstances, for up to two years). Those at risk of disqualification due to the accumulation of penalty points are frequently referred to by the courts as 'totters'.

20.4   Certain grounds are specifically excluded from what a court may consider to be 'mitigating circumstances' (see further below), one of which is

145

'hardship other than exceptional hardship'. 'Exceptional hardship' is therefore a level of hardship that entitles a court to consider it a mitigating circumstance such as to justify a departure from the normal approach to disqualification provided for by the legislation.

SPECIAL REASONS

20.5   'Special reasons' is a term not defined by statute, but is generally accepted to be a reason:

> '... that is special to the facts which constitute the offence. It is, in other words, a mitigating or extenuating circumstance, not amounting in law to a defence to the charge, yet directly connected with the commission of the offence and one which the court ought properly to take into consideration when imposing punishment. A circumstance peculiar to the offender as distinguished from the offence is not a "special reason" within the exception.'[1]

20.6   While some earlier decisions suggested that a relatively trivial offence, or one involving a minor degree of culpability on the part of the offender, may be capable of satisfying the definition, that is no longer the case following *Nicholson v Brown*[2], in which the court concluded that it:

> '... would not accept the proposition that if a man is guilty ... he can be excused endorsement of his licence on the basis of special reasons merely because it was not a bad case, or merely because the degree of blameworthiness was slight ... the line must be drawn firmly at guilt or innocence ... If the defendant is guilty, then the consequences of endorsement of the licence must follow, unless there is some special reason properly to be treated as such, not such a matter as that the offence was not a serious one.'

20.7   As one would expect, the onus of establishing special reasons is on the defendant, and the standard of proof is on the balance of probabilities. The case law establishes that evidence must be called in support of the defendant's case; it is not sufficient to rely simply on submissions. Advance notice of such evidence should, as a matter of good practice, be provided to the prosecution so that they have the opportunity of calling evidence in rebuttal[3].

---

1   *R v Crossen* [1939] 1 NI 106.
2   [1974] RTR 177.
3   *DPP v O'Connor* [1992] RTR 66.

20.8 Each case tends to be acutely fact-specific, but there are a number of previous cases which shed some light on what circumstances have and have not satisfied the test for special reasons. By way of example, circumstances found to amount to special reasons include:

(i) Driving for a short distance, particularly at the request of a third party, and in circumstances where the defendant was unlikely to be brought into contact with, and be a danger to, other road users[4].

(ii) The defendant's drinks being laced with alcohol without his knowledge, coupled with the fact that, but for the 'lacing' of the drinks, the defendant would have been under the prescribed limit. This almost always requires support from an expert witness to confirm that it was the amount of alcohol in the laced drinks that put the motorist over the drink drive limit[5].

(iii) The defendant unintentionally committing the offence of driving without insurance because they have been misled by their insurance company or by someone else telling them that they were insured, for example where a wife or husband has been innocently misled by their partner. However, the defendant's belief that they were insured, no matter how honestly held, can only amount to a special reason if there were reasonable grounds for that belief[6].

(iv) The fact that the defendant committed the offence when responding to a genuine emergency. It is possible that responding to a genuine emergency might, in fact, amount to a complete defence of necessity or duress of circumstances. However, in order to establish emergency as a basis for arguing special reasons, it must first be shown that there was no alternative option to driving and that the defendant had explored every reasonable alternative before deciding to drive.

(v) Driving whilst disqualified when the defendant did not know that they were disqualified and had no good reason to know that they were disqualified.

20.9 Conversely, the following situations have been held not to be capable of amounting to special reasons:

(i) Perhaps obviously, that the defendant is of good character and has a good driving record, or that they and their family will suffer hardship as a result of the penalty[7].

---

4   *Reay v Young* [1949] 1 All ER 1102.
5   *Pugsley v Hunter* [1973] RTR 284.
6   *Rennison v Knowler* [1948] 1 KB 488 and, more recently, *R (on the application of Alma) v DPP* [2009] EWCA Crim 2703.
7   *Whittal v Kirby* [1946] 2 All ER 552.

(ii)   The fact that the defendant requires a driving licence for their employment which provides a public benefit.

(iii)   The triviality of the offence[8].

(iv)   The defendant being marginally over the drink drive limit[9].

20.10   It is important to note that, even where a court makes a finding of special reasons, it does not follow that it must not disqualify or endorse; it retains a discretion as to whether to do so or not.

MITIGATING CIRCUMSTANCES

20.11   As stated above, 'mitigating circumstances' only fall to be considered when a court is faced with the issue of disqualification under the penalty points provisions, and where disqualification must ordinarily follow:

> '… unless the court is satisfied, having regard to all the circumstances, that there are grounds for mitigating the normal consequences of the conviction.' (Road Traffic Offenders Act 1988 ('RTOA 1988'), s 35(1))

20.12   This enables the court to take into account circumstances relating to the defendant, as opposed to those more restrictively defined as special reasons; however, importantly, section 35(4) of the RTOA 1988 states that none of the following circumstances can be taken into account:

(a)   any that are alleged to make the offence or any of the offences not a serious one;

(b)   hardship, other than exceptional hardship; and

(c)   any circumstances taken into account by a court when the offender escaped disqualification or was disqualified for less than the minimum period on a previous occasion within the three years preceding the current conviction.

20.13   Importantly, the practical effect of the first of these three exclusions is that any argument directed to the nature of the offence (as opposed to circumstances relating to the offender) needs to be advanced under the 'special reasons' category for not disqualifying, not as a 'mitigating circumstance'.

---

8   *Nicholson v Brown* [1974] RTR 177.
9   *Delaroy-Hall v Tadman* [1969] 2 QB 208.

EXCEPTIONAL HARDSHIP

20.14 So far as hardship is concerned, under section 35(4)(b) of the RTOA 1988, it is only 'exceptional' hardship that can be relied upon to avoid the consequences of disqualification as a totter. As with special reasons, there is no statutory definition as to what constitutes exceptional hardship, and every case will need to be examined on its own merits. What is clear from the Magistrates' Sentencing Guidelines is that the hardship has to be something greater than that inevitably endured as a result of disqualification. The court will require evidence of hardship of a serious kind, which is likely to be one which results in a considerable adverse effect on the defendant's business, employees or family members.

20.15 As a matter of practice, the courts are highly unlikely to find that exceptional hardship exists where the consequences of disqualification are simply that the offender will have to fulfil his travel commitments by resorting to other means of transport. However, if others would be adversely affected in this way, the argument becomes more compelling, depending on the circumstances.

20.16 Loss of employment is another issue that the courts frequently have to consider. In itself, loss of employment is unlikely to amount to exceptional hardship, as it is an inevitable consequence of a driving ban for many people. Whether it does meet the test will depend upon the individual circumstances of the case and, importantly, on the effect it is likely to have on others. Where it is capable of impacting on the defendant's religious, political, family or cultural life, or results in a dramatic downturn in their family's living standards, different considerations apply and the practitioner may find some of the observations in the Judicial College *Equal Treatment Bench Book*, particularly at chapter 11 ('Social Exclusion and Poverty'), a useful resource in this regard.

20.17 As with special reasons, the onus of establishing mitigating circumstances, be they exceptional hardship or otherwise, is on the defendant, and evidence must be called to satisfy the court that such circumstances exist. If the defendant fails, the court must disqualify the offender for the statutory minimum term concerned. If they succeed, penalty points will still be applied to their licence, but they will either not be disqualified or be disqualified for a shorter term than the statutory minimum.

20.18 The third exclusion, specified in section 35(4)(c) of the RTOA 1988, caters for the situation where an offender has previously successfully advanced similar mitigating circumstances in order to avoid the statutory minimum disqualification. Once particular mitigating circumstances have been successfully relied upon to establish exceptional hardship, the offender cannot rely on these circumstances again within the same three-year period. This prevents repeat offenders from running the same arguments in order to retain their driving licences. Such instances will be comparatively rare and, where they potentially arise, the practitioner will need to obtain a copy of the court register for the previous hearing concerned in order to establish the extent to which the record reflects similar mitigating circumstances. As with all situations under this heading, the burden of proof lies with the defendant, who will need to call evidence to support their case.

Chapter 21

Penalty points

George Joseph

PENALTY POINTS AND ENDORSEMENT OF A DRIVING LICENCE

21.1   Penalty points are imposed on a driver's licence when they are convicted of an offence involving 'obligatory endorsement'. When this happens, the court makes an order for the driver's licence and record to be marked with the particulars or details of the conviction and the number of penalty points imposed as punishment. This procedure is codified in sections 44 and 44A of the Road Traffic Offenders Act 1988 ('RTOA 1988').

21.2   For relatively minor offences, the penalty points are the real punishment. Common examples in this category include failing to comply with traffic conditions and speeding. Anyone who accumulates 12 or more penalty points within a relevant period of time is automatically disqualified as a 'totter', unless exceptions apply.

21.3   The number of penalty points imposed will depend on the type of offence and its seriousness. Some offences carry a fixed number of points, whilst others allow the court greater discretion. The penalty points for each offence are outlined in Chapter 23.

21.4   The time period over which penalty points remain 'active' on your licence depends upon the offence. The points imposed for less serious offences, such as speeding, remain on the licence for four years from the date of the offence. However, they are only taken into account by the court during the first three years. The endorsement for serious offences (which almost always result in disqualification), such as drink or drug driving, remains on the licence for 11 years from the date of conviction rather than the date of the offence.

21.5   When you attend court for an offence which carries penalty points, you may hear the term 'totter' or 'totting up'. This is a colloquial term which the court and lawyers use to refer to the situation in which an individual has accumulated 12 or more penalty points. This will usually result in the driver being disqualified from driving for a minimum of six months under section 35 of the RTOA 1988.

21.6   Although the starting point under section 35 is automatic disqualification, an 'exceptional hardship' argument can be advanced (see Chapter 20), which has the potential to avert immediate disqualification. The only other exception to the six-month minimum rule arises where a driver has been subject to a previous disqualification of 56 days or more within the last three years, or two years if the driver has had two 56-day disqualifications. If this is the case, the minimum period of disqualification is increased to 12 months.

21.7   The number of penalty points imposed should reflect the seriousness of the offence. The sentencing guidelines provide a sliding scale of suggested penalty points according to the seriousness of the offence. This is most apparent in cases involving speeding, where the penalty points increase according to how far over the speed limit the driver was. Careless driving, which may well be more serious, carries a risk of discretionary disqualification and a range of 3 to 11 penalty points.

21.8   The seriousness of the offences and, therefore, the number of points imposed will depend upon various factors such as speed, length of improper driving, volume of traffic, and the risk posed to pedestrians and other road users. The more acute the aggravating features, the greater the number of penalty points imposed. This is apparent from the Sentencing Council guideline for speeding offences[1].

21.9   If a driver is disqualified as a result of accumulating 12 or more penalty points, their DVLA record will be 'wiped clean'. Therefore, when they return to driving, they will not have any active penalty points on their licence. But they should not make the mistake of thinking that it is as though the points never existed. The court will continue to be privy to all of the details of any previous penalty points, regardless of how old they are.

21.10   Where a driver is convicted on the same occasion of more than one offence, under either section 34 or section 35 of the RTOA 1988, only one disqualification will apply. However, determining the period of disqualification can only be done by the court on a case-by-case basis. Many drivers will come to court with a combination of point and other driving-based offences on their

---

1   www.sentencingcouncil.org.uk/offences/magistrates-court/item/speeding-revised-2017.

licence, and so each case can only be dealt with after having considered all the information provided.

DISQUALIFICATION

Obligatory

21.11   Some offences require mandatory disqualification as per section 34 of the RTOA 1988. In these cases, the court must order the driver to be disqualified for a period of not less than 12 months, unless special reasons apply. If special reasons are found, disqualification can be for a shorter period or not imposed at all.

21.12   As with penalty points, the minimum period of disqualification increases depending upon the seriousness of the offence. Section 34(4) of the RTOA 1988 sets out those offences for which the minimum period of disqualification is two years. These include manslaughter and causing death or serious injury by dangerous driving[2]. The disqualification period rises again to a minimum of three years where the driver has had two or more periods of disqualification of 56 days or more within the three years preceding the commission of the offence. Likewise, a second or subsequent conviction for an offence of drink or drug driving carries a minimum disqualification of three years if it is committed within 10 years of the same offence.

21.13   If the period of disqualification is for 56 days or more, the driver will need to apply for a new driving licence before they can drive again. The court also has the discretion to order an offender to re-take their driving test before the licence can be restored. Moreover, those convicted of serious offences, such as dangerous driving, are required to undertake an extended re-test.

21.14   At sentence, the magistrates can offer a drink-drive rehabilitation course which, if accepted and completed by the defendant, will reduce the ban by one quarter. The usher at court will be able to provide a copy of a leaflet outlining the courses. A decision will need to be made before the hearing is concluded as to whether the driver will undertake the course. The courses are not free, but the cost is relatively modest. There are some situations in which the course is not available, namely where the driver:

(a)   is still within the probationary period for new drivers (first two years of holding a driving licence);

---

2   As has been set out in Chapter 15, the minimum disqualification period for causing death by dangerous driving is five years for offences committed on or after 28 June 2022.

(b) is under 17 years of age; or

(c) has already completed the course for a separate offence within the last three years.

21.15 The effect of a disqualification is that the driver's licence is treated as being revoked from the beginning of the disqualification. It is important that a driver at risk of disqualification does not drive to court. If they are disqualified, they will not be able to drive home!

Discretionary

21.16 Where disqualification is discretionary for a single offence, and the driver does not fall foul of the totting up provisions, the court is unlikely to conclude, except in more serious cases, that disqualification is appropriate. Nevertheless, driving without insurance, or failing to stop after an accident, can be punished by disqualification even if penalty points are usually imposed.

21.17 The decision to disqualify has to be appropriate according to the facts of the case. In *R v Callister*[3], the defendant had stolen a car and received a sentence of imprisonment. However, the Court of Appeal quashed the disqualification order imposed. It was held that it was not appropriate to order disqualification in a case where the offender had not been guilty of bad driving, persistent motoring offences, or using the car to commit a crime.

21.18 The situation in which the court had to decide between imposing penalty points and a discretionary disqualification was considered in *Jones v DPP*[4]. The offender had 11 penalty points on his licence and had then been caught travelling at between 94 and 101mph on a road subject to a 60mph speed limit. It was held that the proper approach was to first consider discretionary disqualification under section 34(2) of the RTOA 1988, taking into account the driver's whole driving record, before turning to the question of penalty points. It seems that the court reached this conclusion on the basis that there may be cases in which a disqualification period of more than six months, which would automatically follow for a totter, is appropriate.

21.19 If the driver attends court for an offence where disqualification is discretionary, but the same driver has 12 or more penalty points on their licence, those points remain on their record until they either:

(a) expire under the three-year rule; or

3   [1993] RTR 70.
4   [2001] RTR 8.

(b)   the driver is disqualified under section 35 of the RTOA 1988, which results in the points being expunged. However, the number of points is still taken into account when making the decision as to whether the driver should be disqualified.

21.20   In cases where the magistrates' court is considering imposing a disqualification, and the driver fails to attend court, it is usual practice for the court to adjourn the hearing. This is to enable the driver or their solicitor to make representations as to why disqualification would not be appropriate, and to ensure that the driver knows that they have been disqualified. If the driver fails to attend without proper reason, a warrant will be issued by the court to compel attendance at the next hearing.

SUSPENSION PENDING APPEAL

21.21   A driver who is disqualified by the magistrates' court under section 34 or section 35 of the RTOA 1988 may appeal the decision of the lower court to the Crown Court. If the driver does decide to appeal, a request should be made to the magistrates' court to suspend the disqualification under section 39 of the RTOA 1988, pending the appeal.

21.22   Simply filing and serving the appeal forms is not sufficient; the court needs to be specifically asked to consider the provision under section 39. This is an entirely separate application that must be made. If it is not, the disqualification will remain in place. Section 39 gives the court the power to suspend a disqualification 'if it thinks fit'. Although this language may sound vague, the considerations that the court will take into account are fairly straightforward. These factors will include:

(a)   the prospects of successfully appealing the decision of the lower court;

(b)   the length of time until the appeal will be heard; and

(c)   any hardship that may be suffered in the interim period until the appeal can be heard.

21.23   It is usual for the section 39 argument to be made after sentence, to alert the court to the fact that there will be an appeal against the decision, but the application does not necessarily need to be made on the same day. An application to suspend disqualification pending appeal can be made to the court on a different occasion and it does not need to be made to the same bench of magistrates. Whatever bench hears the application will consider all the arguments before deciding whether or not to suspend.

LOSS OF LICENCE WITHIN THE FIRST TWO YEARS[5]

21.24   Newly qualified drivers are subject to a probationary period of two years commencing from the day on which they become a qualified driver (Road Traffic (New Drivers) Act 1995, s 1).

21.25   If a driver accumulates six or more penalty points, within the probationary period, a notice will be sent to them revoking their licence. However, special reasons may still be argued to prevent the licence from being revoked.

21.26   Where a licence is revoked under this provision, the holder must retake their driving test in order to be eligible for a new licence. Importantly, after passing this test, no probationary period is attached. This prevents offenders from being in a perpetual cycle of having to reapply for their licence.

21.27   If a new driver, subject to the probationary period, appeals against the conviction or penalty points that led to their licence being revoked, their licence will be temporarily restored pending the determination of the appeal. If the appeal is successful, the driver will remain on their probationary period, and any penalty points which led to the initial revocation will remain effective for the standard three-year period from the date of the commission of the offence. It is important to note that, in the context of probationary drivers, revocation of a licence does not result in the licence being wiped clean, as would be the case for a driver not subject to the probationary period.

---

5   This topic is also covered in Chapter 4.

Chapter 22

Mandatory disqualification

Susan Cavender

22.1   The previous chapter was concerned with the implications of accumulating penalty points. This chapter focuses on cases in which disqualification is mandatory. Drivers can lose their licence as a result of either discretionary or mandatory disqualification. In the case of the former, the decision as to whether to disqualify at all, and for how long, is determined at a hearing by the magistrates or by a Crown Court judge.

22.2   Disqualification is mandatory in three sets of circumstances:

(i)   For various offences, most obviously and frequently for driving with excess alcohol.

(ii)   As a 'totter' when 12 or more penalty points are accumulated in three years.

(iii)   For new drivers, if more than six penalty points are accumulated in the first two years of driving (this is 'revocation', not technically a 'disqualification' but has the same effect – a new test must be taken).

22.3   In the case of drink-driving, where disqualification is automatic for 12 months or more, the court will ask whether a defendant wishes to reduce the length of ban by taking a drink-drive rehabilitation course. A list of local course providers is set out in a leaflet handed to the defendant prior to sentence, and they can select one from the list to be specified in the sentence as a route to reduction in the length of the ban.

22.4   Disqualification cannot generally be imposed unless the driver is present, though this requirement can be waived in certain circumstances, as per section 11 of the Magistrates' Courts Act 1980. Usually, if disqualification is anticipated, the case will be adjourned and the driver notified of the new date, and/or a warrant issued for their arrest. If that adjournment does not do the trick, it is open to the court on the next occasion to disqualify in the defendant's absence. This is referred to in the Sentencing Council guidelines[1].

---

1   www.sentencingcouncil.org.uk/explanatory-material/magistrates-court/item/road-traffic-offences-disqualification/7-disqualification-in-the-offenders-absence.

22.5   Obligatory disqualification can only be avoided by pleading 'special reasons', or if an order is made under the Mental Health Act 1983 provisions, when the finding that the defendant 'did the act' does not amount to a formal conviction, or in certain cases of aiding and abetting an obligatorily disqualifiable offence.

22.6   Mandatory disqualification is usually for a minimum of 12 months but increases to a minimum of two years[2] in cases of:

- manslaughter;

- death by dangerous driving;

- death by careless driving when under the influence of drink or drugs; or

- causing death (or serious injury) by driving whilst disqualified, if the offender has been disqualified at least twice in the past three years, and for at least eight weeks on each occasion.

22.7   Disqualification is raised to three years if an offender is convicted of one of the following offences for the second time within the 10 years preceding the commission of the offence (Road Traffic Offenders Act 1988 ('RTOA 1988'), s 34(3)):

- causing death by careless driving when under the influence of drink or drugs;

- driving or attempting to drive while unfit;

- driving or attempting to drive with excess alcohol;

- driving or attempting to drive with concentration of specified controlled drug above specified limit; or

- failing to provide a specimen (drive/attempting to drive).

22.8   Mandatory disqualification is governed by section 34 of the RTOA 1988 which stipulates that:

> 'Where a person is convicted of an offence involving obligatory disqualification, the court *must* order him to be disqualified for such period not less than twelve months as the court thinks fit *unless* the court for *special reasons* thinks fit to order him to be disqualified for a shorter period or not to order him to be disqualified.' (emphasis added)

---

2   And up to five years for some offences committed on or after 28 June 2022 – see the table in Chapter 23.

22.9   Special reasons are discussed in Chapter 20, which outlines how these provisions can be invoked when attempting to avoid mandatory disqualification.

22.10   It should be noted that mandatory disqualification is often specified as 'disqualification until an extended test has been passed'. In these cases, the driving licence is not automatically returned or re-activated at the end of the disqualification period. Instead, the disqualification *only* ends when an extended test is taken and passed. Simply waiting out the 12 months and starting to drive again constitutes a further offence – a fact which many fail to appreciate, and they are then prosecuted for driving whilst disqualified if they drive without having taken the extended test.

22.11   For a 'totter' who has accumulated 12 or more penalty points during a three-year period, the points are calculated from the date of the offence (not the date that it came to court), and the minimum period of disqualification is six months, unless there are 'mitigating circumstances' which have to be argued before the court.

22.12   The ban can last for:

- six months, if you get 12 or more penalty points within three years;

- 12 months, if you get a second disqualification within three years; and

- two years, if you get a third disqualification within three years.

22.13   If disqualified for 56 days (eight weeks) or more, the licence is automatically revoked and a driver must apply for a new licence before driving again.

22.14   Disqualification for less than eight weeks is much less onerous and there is no need to apply for a new licence before driving again. Driving licence records can easily be viewed on the government website[3].

22.15   In very limited circumstances, it is possible to apply to the court to have the disqualification period reduced. The court has the discretion to reduce the period for a 'good reason', but this can only be done:

- after two years where the ban was for under four years, or

- after half the period where the ban was between four and 10 years, or

- after five years if the ban was for 10 years or more.

3   www.gov.uk/view-driving-licence.

22.16   If disqualification is reduced, a new licence must be applied for or, where a re-test is required, a new provisional licence obtained prior to taking the new full test. Driving can only resume once the required test, or extended test, has been passed and the fresh licence obtained.

22.17   The DVLA will usually send a reminder 56 days before a disqualification is due to end, to inform the driver that a new licence needs to be applied for. The gov.uk website is full of useful information about how to apply for a new licence after disqualification.

22.18   High-risk offenders are required to pass a medical examination with one of the DVLA's appointed doctors before being able to drive again. 'High-risk' offenders are those who fall into the following categories:

- Those who have been convicted of two drink driving offences within 10 years.

- Those caught driving with an alcohol reading of at least 87.5 micrograms of alcohol per 100 millilitres (ml) of breath, 200 milligrams (mg) of alcohol per 100 ml of blood, or 267.5 mg of alcohol per 100 ml of urine.

- Those who refused to give the police a sample of breath, blood or urine to test for alcohol.

- Those who refused to allow a sample of blood to be tested for alcohol (for example, if it was taken whilst the offender was unconscious).

22.19   In these cases, a D27PH renewal form will arrive 90 days before the disqualification ends. It needs to be completed and sent to DVLA. The DVLA will then send out the details of an approved doctor with whom an appointment can be made, and a fee will need to be paid for the medical examination.

22.20   It is also important to note the potential effects of sections 163 and 164 of the Sentencing Act 2020. Following their recent enactment, these two sections enable the courts to disqualify drivers for any endorsable offence. Moreover, section 34 gives the court the power to disqualify in cases where the vehicle has been used to commit an indictable offence which carries imprisonment of two years or more. In these circumstances, 'use of the vehicle' arises where the vehicle was used to commit or facilitate the offence. This provision enables the court to disqualify the driver of a get-away vehicle in a robbery, individuals involved in 'road rage' offences, or someone who assaults their victim by deliberately driving into them.

Chapter 23

Summary tables of road traffic offences

DRIVING OFFENCES

23.1

Offence	Mode of trial	Maximum sentence	Penalty points	Notes
Causing death by dangerous driving	Indictable	Life imprisonment (for offences committed on or after 28 June 2022)	Mandatory disqualification	Minimum disqualification of 5 years (for offences committed on or after 28 June 2022). Offender required to undertake extended re-test.
Causing death by careless driving under the influence of drink or drugs	Indictable	Life imprisonment (for offences committed on or after 28 June 2022)	Mandatory disqualification	Minimum disqualification of 5 years (for offences committed on or after 28 June 2022). Offender required to undertake extended re-test.
Causing death by careless driving	Either way	5 years' imprisonment	Mandatory disqualification	Special reasons may be found to prevent disqualification, in which case 3–11 points are imposed.

Offence	Mode of trial	Maximum sentence	Penalty points	Notes
Causing death by driving: unlicensed, disqualified or uninsured drivers	Either way	2 years' imprisonment	Mandatory disqualification	Special reasons may be found to prevent disqualification, in which case 3–11 points are imposed.
Causing serious injury by dangerous driving	Either way	5 years' imprisonment	Mandatory disqualification	Minimum disqualification of 2 years. Offender required to undertake extended re-test.
Causing serious injury by careless driving	Either way	2 years' imprisonment	Mandatory disqualification	
Causing injury by wanton or furious driving	Indictable	2 years' imprisonment	Discretionary disqualification or 3–11 points	
Dangerous driving	Either way	2 years' imprisonment	Mandatory disqualification	Offender required to undertake extended re-test. Must disqualify for at least 2 years if the offender has had two or more disqualifications for at least 56 days in the preceding 3 years.
Careless driving	Summary	Unlimited fine	Discretionary disqualification or 3–9 points	
Drive whilst disqualified	Summary	6 months' imprisonment	Discretionary disqualification or 6 points	Although this is a summary offence, it can be tried in the Crown Court if it is linked to an either-way or indictable offence.

Offence	Mode of trial	Maximum sentence	Penalty points	Notes
Drive whilst over the prescribed drug limit	Summary	6 months' imprisonment	Mandatory disqualification	Must disqualify for at least 2 years if the offender has had two or more disqualifications for at least 56 days in the preceding 3 years. This increases to at least 3 years if the offender has been convicted of a relevant offence in the preceding 10 years.
Being in charge of a vehicle whilst over the prescribed drug limit	Summary	3 months' imprisonment	Discretionary disqualification or 10 points	
Drive whilst over the prescribed alcohol limit	Summary	6 months' imprisonment	Mandatory disqualification	Must disqualify for at least 2 years if the offender has had two or more disqualifications for at least 56 days in the preceding 3 years. This increases to at least 3 years if the offender has been convicted of a relevant offence in the preceding 10 years.
Being in charge of a vehicle whilst over the prescribed alcohol limit	Summary	3 months' imprisonment	Discretionary disqualification or 10 points	
Fail to cooperate with roadside breath test	Summary	Level 3 fine	4	

Offence	Mode of trial	Maximum sentence	Penalty points	Notes
Fail to stop after an accident or fail to report an accident	Summary	6 months' imprisonment	Discretionary disqualification or 5–10 points	
Drive after the refusal or revocation of a driving licence on medical grounds	Summary	6 months' imprisonment	Discretionary disqualification or 3–6 points	
No insurance	Summary	Unlimited fine	Discretionary disqualification or 6–8 points	
Speeding	Summary	Level 3 fine Level 4 fine (offence on motorway)	Discretionary disqualification or 3–6 points	
Drive otherwise than in accordance with a licence (where could be covered)	Summary	Level 3 fine	-	
Drive otherwise than in accordance with a licence	Summary	Level 3 fine	3–6 points	Offence aggravated where no licence has ever been held.
Dangerous parking	Summary	Level 3 fine	3 points	
Pelican/zebra crossing contravention	Summary	Level 3 fine	3 points	
Fail to comply with a traffic prevention sign (eg red light, stop sign, no entry sign)	Summary	Level 3 fine	3 points	

Offence	Mode of trial	Maximum sentence	Penalty points	Notes
Fail to comply with traffic movement sign (eg give way sign, keep left sign)	Summary	Level 3 fine	-	
Fail to comply with police constable directing traffic	Summary	Level 3 fine	3 points	
Fail to stop when required by a police constable	Summary	Level 5 fine (mechanically propelled vehicle) Level 3 fine (bicycle)	-	
Use of mobile phone whilst driving	Summary	Level 3 fine	6 points	
Seat belt offences	Summary	Level 2 fine	-	
Fail to use appropriate child car seat	Summary	Level 2 fine	-	
Drive in reverse or wrong way on slip road	Summary	Level 4 fine	3 points	
Drive in reverse or wrong way on motorway	Summary	Level 4 fine	3 points	
Drive off carriageway (central reservation or hard shoulder)	Summary	Level 4 fine	3 points	
Make a U-turn on motorway	Summary	Level 4 fine	3 points	

Offence	Mode of trial	Maximum sentence	Penalty points	Notes
Drive in prohibited lane	Summary	Level 4 fine	3 points	

DISHONESTY OFFENCES

23.2

Offence	Mode of trial	Maximum sentence	Penalty points	Notes
Taking a vehicle without consent	Summary	6 months' imprisonment	Discretionary disqualification	
Aggravated vehicle taking	Either way	2 years' imprisonment	Mandatory disqualification	Must disqualify for at least 2 years if the offender has had two or more disqualifications for at least 56 days in the preceding 3 years.
Theft (including vehicle theft)	Either way	7 years' imprisonment	-	As with other dishonesty offences, the court has a general discretion to disqualify the offender from driving.
Interfering with a vehicle	Summary	3 months' imprisonment	-	General discretion to disqualify from driving.
Vehicle licence/ registration fraud	Either way	2 years' imprisonment	-	General discretion to disqualify from driving.

VEHICLE OFFENCES

23.3

Offence	Mode of trial	Maximum sentence	Penalty points	Notes
Defective brakes	Summary	Level 5 fine (goods vehicle) Level 4 fine (other circumstances)	3 points	
Defective steering	Summary	Level 5 fine (goods vehicle) Level 4 fine (other circumstances)	3 points	
Defective tyres	Summary	Level 5 fine (goods vehicle) Level 4 fine (other circumstances)	3 points	
Defective lights	Summary	Level 3 fine	-	
Exhaust emission	Summary	Level 4 fine (goods vehicle) Level 3 fine (other circumstances)	-	
Condition of the vehicle involving a danger of injury	Summary	Level 5 fine (goods vehicle) Level 4 fine (other circumstances)	3 points	Must disqualify for at least 6 months if the offender has one or more previous convictions for the same offence within 3 years.
Number of passengers, or manner carried, involving danger of injury	Summary	Level 5 fine	3 points	Must disqualify for at least 6 months if the offender has one or more previous convictions for the same offence within 3 years.

Offence	Mode of trial	Maximum sentence	Penalty points	Notes
Weight, position or distribution of load, or manner in which load secured, involving danger of injury	Summary	Level 5 fine	3 points	Must disqualify for at least 6 months if the offender has one or more previous convictions for the same offence within 3 years.
Position of load, or manner in which load secured (not involving danger)	Summary	Level 4 fine	-	
Overloading/ exceeding axle weight	Summary	Level 5 fine	-	
No operators' licence	Summary	Level 4 fine (public service vehicle) Level 5 fine (goods vehicle)	-	
Speed limiter not used or incorrectly calibrated	Summary	Level 4 fine	-	

DOCUMENT OFFENCES

23.4

Offence	Mode of trial	Maximum sentence	Penalty points	Notes
Fail to give information as to driver's identity	Summary	Level 3 fine	6 points	For limited companies, penalty points cannot be imposed.

Offence	Mode of trial	Maximum sentence	Penalty points	Notes
Fail to produce insurance certificate	Summary	Level 4 fine	-	
Fail to produce test certificate	Summary	Level 3 fine	-	
No excise licence	Summary	Level 3 fine	-	
Fail to notify change of ownership to DVLA	Summary	Level 3 fine	-	
No test certificate	Summary	Level 3 fine	-	
Fail to disclose medical condition	Summary	Level 3 fine	-	

GOODS VEHICLE OFFENCES

23.5

Offence	Mode of trial	Maximum sentence	Penalty points	Notes
No goods vehicle planting certificate	Summary	Level 3 fine	-	
No goods vehicle test certificate	Summary	Level 4 fine	-	
Exceed permitted driving time or duty period	Summary	Level 4 fine	-	

Offence	Mode of trial	Maximum sentence	Penalty points	Notes
Fail to keep or return written record sheets	Summary	Level 4 fine	-	
Falsify or alter records with intent to deceive	Either way	2 years' imprisonment	-	
Tachograph not used or not working	Summary	Level 5 fine	-	

Part 6

Miscellaneous

Chapter 24

An introduction to goods vehicles

Andrew Banks

24.1   There are specific rules for the drivers of heavy goods vehicles over and above those which relate to the typical road user. These rules are strict, and the implications of breaking them are severe, so it is important to remain up to date with developments in this sometimes complex area.

DRIVER'S HOURS RULES

Introduction

24.2   The majority of vehicles driven for the carriage of goods are required to abide by driver's hours rules. These regulate the amount of time a driver can drive a goods vehicle before requiring a break or rest. The rules also set maximum periods of driving time.

24.3   There are two sets of driver's hours rules: EU/AETR[1] rules; and domestic hours rules. Although the UK has now left the EU, the EU/AETR rules still apply.

EU/AETR driver's hours rules

24.4   The EU/AETR rules apply to most journeys by goods vehicles in the UK. Although the EU rules will apply in the majority of cases, there are several exemptions.

24.5   The most significant of these exemptions relates to vehicles (or combinations of vehicles) with a maximum permissible mass not exceeding 7.5 tonnes which are only used for specific purposes.

---

1   European Agreement Concerning the Work of Crews of Vehicles Engaged in International Road Transport ('AETR').

24.6 These specific purposes include:

- carrying materials, equipment or machinery for the driver's use in the course of their work; or

- delivering goods produced on a craft basis.

24.7 In both cases, this must only be:

- within a 100 km radius from the base of the undertaking;

- on condition that driving the vehicle does *not* constitute the driver's main activity; and

- on condition that the transport is *not* carried out for hire or reward.

24.8 Carrying materials, equipment or machinery would apply to tradesmen such as electricians or builders carrying tools or materials for their own use. The terms 'material or equipment' covers not only tools and instruments, but also goods which are required for the performance of the work involved in the main activity of the driver.

24.9 Another important exemption relates to vehicles (or combinations of vehicles with a maximum permissible mass not exceeding 7.5 tonnes) used for the non-commercial carriage of goods. This would cover the carriage by road, but not for hire or reward, or on the driver's own account and without payment of any kind, which is not linked to a professional or commercial activity – in other words, taking goods on a completely non-commercial basis, out of the goodness of the driver's heart.

24.10 One of the main requirements of journeys in which the EU rules apply is that the hours driven must be recorded on a tachograph which can be analogue or, as is more common now, a digital or smart tachograph recorder.

24.11 The rules dictating the periods over which one can drive a goods vehicle are available online[2]; in essence, the rules amount to the following.

Breaks from driving

24.12 A break is any period during which a driver may not carry out any driving, or any other work, and which is used exclusively for recuperation. A break may be taken in a moving vehicle, provided no other work is undertaken, so the driver may take a break by resting in the cab whilst parked, but that time cannot be used to complete timesheets which would count as 'work'.

---

2 www.gov.uk/drivers-hours/eu-rules.

24.13   A break of no less than 45 minutes must be taken during a four-and-a-half-hour period of driving. The break can be divided into two periods – the first being at least 15 minutes long, and the second at least 30 minutes – taken over the four and a half hours.

Daily driving

24.14   Daily driving time is either the total accumulated driving time between the end of one daily rest period and the beginning of the following daily rest period, or the total accumulated driving time between a daily rest period and a weekly rest period (or vice versa). A driver is permitted to drive a maximum of nine hours per day, although this is extendable to up to 10 hours twice a week.

Weekly driving

24.15   The maximum period of driving time allowed in respect of weekly driving is 56 hours. This applies to a fixed week which starts at 00.00 hours on Monday and ends at 24.00 hours on the following Sunday.

Two-weekly driving

24.16   The maximum permissible period of driving in a two-week period is 90 hours.

Daily rest

24.17   A rest is an uninterrupted period during which a driver may freely dispose of their time. This must be for a minimum of 11 hours, which can be reduced to a minimum of nine hours no more than three times between weekly rests. This rest may also be taken in two periods; the first being at least three hours long, and the second at least nine hours long. This would amount to a total of 12 hours' rest in a 24-hour period. The rest must be completed within 24 hours of the end of the last daily or weekly rest period.

24.18   Time working in other employment (including volunteering), when there is an obligation to undertake duties, cannot count as rest and must be counted as duty. Time spent undertaking training, such as the Driver Certificate of Competence, would also amount to duty time and not rest time.

24.19   Daily rest can be taken on a vehicle but that vehicle *must* have suitable sleeping facilities and be stationary.

Multi-manning daily rest

24.20 A daily rest can be reduced to a minimum of nine hours' duration, but this daily rest must be taken within a period of 30 hours that starts from the end of the last daily or weekly rest period. In addition, a nine-hour daily rest is a reduced daily rest period and is subject to a limit of three occasions between weekly rest periods. For the first hour of multi-manning, the presence of another driver is optional, but for the remaining time it is compulsory. It is possible to take split daily rest as part of a multi-manned operation.

Ferry/train daily rest

24.21 A regular daily rest period (of at least 11 hours), or weekly rest periods, may be interrupted no more than twice by other activities of not more than one hour's duration in total, provided that the driver is accompanying a vehicle that is travelling by ferry or train and has access to a sleeper cabin, bunk or couchette. Interrupting a regular weekly rest in this way is also only permitted where the ferry or train leg of the journey is scheduled for eight hours or more.

Weekly rest

24.22 A regular weekly rest of at least 45 hours, or reduced weekly rest of a least 24 hours, must be started no later than at the end of six days (six consecutive 24-hour periods) from the end of the last weekly rest. In any period of two consecutive weeks, a driver must have at least two weekly rests, one of which must be at least 45 hours long. A weekly rest that falls across two weeks may be counted in either week but not both. Any reductions must be compensated in one block by an equivalent rest added to another rest period. This compensatory rest must be for at least nine hours, and take place before the end of the third week following the week in question.

GB DOMESTIC DRIVER'S HOURS RULES

24.23 These rules will apply in many cases where the EU/AETR rules do not apply as a consequence of an exemption. There are some cases where no rules apply and there is no requirement to observe or record driver's hours rules (for example, in cases of a true emergency) but that is outside the ambit of this chapter, and specialist advice should be sought if in doubt.

24.24 Driving is defined as being at the controls of a vehicle for the purposes of controlling its movement, whether it is moving or stationary with the engine running, even for a short period of time. Sitting in grid-locked traffic with the engine running therefore counts as 'driving'.

Daily driving

24.25   In any working day, the maximum amount of driving permitted is 10 hours. The daily driving limit applies to driving on and off the public road. However, off-road driving for the purposes of agriculture, quarrying, forestry, building work or civil engineering is included as duty rather than driving time. The driving day is defined as being the 24-hour period beginning with the start of duty time.

Daily duty

24.26   In any working day, the maximum amount of duty permitted is 11 hours. A driver is exempt from the daily duty limit of 11 hours on any working day on which they do not drive. Moreover, a driver who does not drive for more than four hours on each day of the week is exempt from the daily duty limit for the whole week. As with the EU/AETR rules, a week is defined as the period from 00.00 hours on a Monday to 24.00 hours the following Sunday.

24.27   Duty means, in the case of an employee driver, being on duty (whether driving or otherwise) for anyone who employs them as a driver. This includes all periods of work and driving, but does not include rest or breaks. Employers should also remember that they have additional obligations to ensure that drivers receive adequate rest under health and safety legislation.

24.28   For self-employed drivers, duty means driving a vehicle connected with their business, or doing any other work connected with the vehicle and its load.

24.29   Drivers of certain vehicles are exempt from the duty limit but not the driving limit. These vehicles are goods vehicles, including dual-purpose vehicles, which do not exceed the maximum permitted gross weight of 3.5 tonnes, when used:

- by doctors, dentists, nurses, midwives or vets;

- for any service of inspection, cleaning, maintenance, repair, installation or fitting;

- by commercial travellers when carrying goods (other than personal effects) only for the purpose of soliciting orders;

- by the AA, RAC or RSAC; or

- for cinematography or radio and television broadcasting.

Rest and breaks

24.30   Whilst the GB domestic rules make no specific provision for rest periods or breaks, employers are required, under the Working Time Regulations 1998, to ensure that drivers have 'adequate rest' (which includes adequate breaks). Adequate rest is defined in the regulations as being sufficiently long and continuous to ensure that a driver does not harm themselves, fellow workers, or others, and to ensure that that they do not damage their health in the long or short term. Taking 'adequate rest' means that a driver's personal circumstances need to be considered when scheduling duty and driving periods.

24.31   Drivers of vehicles used for the carriage of goods that require an Operator Licence, and where the daily driving exceeds four hours, must keep written records of their hours of work on a weekly record sheet. Operators are expected to check and sign each weekly record sheet. These can take the form of record books or log books containing weekly record sheets.

FALSIFICATION OF DRIVER'S HOURS RECORDS

24.32   There are a number of serious offences which relate to the falsification of tachograph records, whether those records be analogue or digital. The seriousness of these offences is a consequence of them being a deliberate assault on the purpose underpinning the regulations, which are in place to prevent people from driving whilst fatigued. These offences are triable either way and therefore capable of being sentenced or tried in the magistrates' court or Crown Court.

24.33   Under section 98 of the Transport Act 1968, it is an offence for a person to make, or cause to be made, any written record relating to driver's hours which they know is false or, with the intention to deceive, to alter (or cause to be altered) any such record. For an offence to be committed, the accused must know that the record is false. The mens rea is therefore akin to dishonesty and requires an awareness of a deception of some kind.

24.34   It is also an offence under section 99ZE(1) of the Transport Act 1968 for a person to:

(i)   make or cause to be made any relevant record or entry which they know to be false;

(ii)   alter or cause to be altered any relevant record or entry with the intention to deceive;

(iii)   destroy or hide or cause to be destroyed or hidden any relevant record or entry; or

(iv)   fail to make a relevant record or entry without reasonable excuse, or cause or permit such a failure.

24.35   Under section 99ZE(3) of the Transport Act 1968, it is an offence for a person to:

(i)   record, or cause or permit to be recorded, any data which they know to be false on recording equipment or on a driver card;

(ii)   record, or cause or permit to be recorded, any data which they know to be false on any hard copy of data previously stored on recording equipment or on a driver card;

(iii)   alter, or cause or permit to be altered, any data stored on recording equipment or on a driver card or appearing on any copy of data previously so stored with the intention to deceive;

(iv)   produce anything falsely purporting to be a hard copy of data stored on recording equipment or on a driver card, with the intent to deceive;

(v)   destroy or hide, or cause or permit to be destroyed or hidden, any data stored in compliance with the requirements of the applicable EU rules on recording equipment or on a driver card; or

(vi)   fail to record any data on recording equipment or on a driver card, or to cause or permit such a failure, without reasonable excuse.

24.36   There are additional offences under section 99ZE(6) of the Transport Act 1968. These include offences of production, distribution, installation, advertising or selling any device which is designed to interfere with the proper operation of recording equipment, or which enables the falsification, alteration, destruction or suppression of data stored on such devices. It is also an offence to provide information to someone to assist them in producing such a device.

24.37   It is also an offence contrary to section 97AA of the Transport Act 1968 for a person, with intent to deceive, to forge, to alter or to use any seal on recording equipment installed in, or designed for installation in, a vehicle to which section 97 or section 97ZA of the Act applies. A person forges a seal for the purposes of this offence if they make a false seal in order that it may be used as genuine.

24.38   It is not only individuals who can commit falsification offences. Operators and owners can be prosecuted for permitting the commission of offences. That would apply if they are, or ought reasonably to be, aware of the falsification, or of it being a likelihood, but took no steps to prevent it. There is a requirement that operators holding Goods Vehicle Operator Licences will have systems in place to monitor driver's hours compliance, including assessing and reviewing tachograph records and taking disciplinary action against drivers for non-compliance. The failure to have in place a suitable and effective system is likely to negate any potential defence to a charge of permitting the commission of falsification offences.

SENTENCING GUIDELINES

24.39   The sentencing guidelines for infringements of driver's hours rules are not detailed. The maximum sentence for most driver's hours infringements is a level 4 fine (currently £2,500).

24.40   As a result of the dishonesty involved, offences concerning the falsification of tachographs and driver's hours records are more serious. Most offences will be sent to the Crown Court for trial or sentence; and custodial sentences, which are either immediate or suspended, are not uncommon.

24.41   The maximum sentence for such offences in the magistrates' court is an unlimited fine. In the Crown Court, the maximum sentence is a term of imprisonment of two years. In *R v Saunders*[3], the eight-month prison sentences imposed were upheld by the Court of Appeal, despite the fact that two of the appellants were of previous good character. In dismissing the appeal, the court observed that the defendants had gained financially from the additional hours of work and that the offences had put other road users at risk.

24.42   In addition to being sentenced by the criminal courts, a driver or operator that has committed a driver's hours offence is likely to be required to appear before their regulator, the Traffic Commissioner, at either a driver conduct hearing or, in the case of an operator, a Public Inquiry. It is important to note that a driver who commits such an offence is at real risk of losing their vocational driving licence, and thereby their livelihood, as a consequence of convictions for offences of this nature.

---

3   [2001] EWCA Crim 93.

Chapter 25

Taxis

Susan Cavender

25.1   Taxis, as we all know, are vehicles used to convey fare-paying passengers. As you would expect, this is a heavily regulated area of law with passenger safety at the heart of the various sets of rules. Transport in return for payment is known as 'hire and reward'. Vehicles which undertake such work must have specific insurance to cover them.

25.2   'Hire and reward' is widely defined and can include the provision of courtesy buses (for example, by a hotel or supermarket to transport customers), even where no payment is made. Even acceptance of petrol money by a parent taking 11 children to and from school amounted to a 'systematic carrying of passengers' going beyond social kindness, and therefore amounting to hire and reward, which in turn meant that the vehicle came to be a Public Service Vehicle and became subject to regulation.

25.3   Public Service Vehicles, as regulated by the Public Passenger Vehicles Act 1981, are defined as a motor vehicle adapted to carry more than eight passengers for hire or reward, or for carrying passengers at separate fares as part of a business. These vehicles are not dealt with in this chapter, which is focused on taxis. A taxi is defined as a vehicle used to transport fewer than nine passengers.

25.4   Leaving larger vehicles to one side, there are two separate and entirely distinct categories of taxi – hackney carriages, and private hire vehicles – with entirely separate regulatory regimes for each. For taxi drivers in either category, compliance with the requirements of the licensing regime set by their local authority is essential if they are to continue with their livelihood.

HACKNEY CARRIAGES

25.5   Hackney carriages have been in use for over 200 years, regulated since 1847 by the Town Police Clauses Act designed for horse-drawn carriages. The

25.6 *Taxis*

Transport Act 1985 ('TA 1985') extended the coverage of the 1847 Act so that there are, broadly speaking, now two licensing regimes; the first covering the whole of England and Wales, and the second Greater London.

25.6   The defining feature of hackney carriages is that the cab can be hailed by passengers without pre-booking – typically done by the customer waving them down from the side of the road – and they can park on cab ranks to await customers. The driver must hold a hackney carriage licence.

25.7   Each local authority, through its Public Carriage Office (Transport for London in the capital), can set conditions to cover the type of vehicle, appearance (including colour), number of seats (8 is a maximum), to more specific matters such as the turning circle and luggage space. The number of hackney carriages can be limited by each authority for that area, who will also set the rates of fare. Fares can be a straightforward charge by time, or a complex framework to include different times of day, numbers of passengers, and amounts of luggage.

25.8   Hackney carriage drivers have to pass stringent tests. The 'Knowledge' test for a London cabbie is well known, but the most important element is that of being a 'fit and proper person'. These can be wide-ranging requirements and each authority can set their own test. The number of licences available in any local authority area can be limited by the authority, but only if it can be shown that there is 'no significant unmet demand' (TA 1985, s 16).

25.9   Once a fare has been accepted, both the driver and the passenger are contractually obliged to complete the journey and pay the fare within a maximum distance set by the local authority. There are only limited reasons for a driver to refuse to accept a fare if plying for hire. Once a ride commences, if the passenger turns out to have insufficient money for the fare, there are two options: the driver can either complete the journey at the lower fare, or terminate the journey prematurely.

25.10   Hackney carriages can be hired to more than one person at a time, with each person paying their own share of the fare (TA 1985, s 10).

25.11   Inner London has its own rules for hackney carriages, and this book does not deal in detail with that aspect of taxi law. If further details are required, the Transport for London website provides comprehensive information[1].

25.12   The following is a short summary of the applicable legislation:

---

1   tfl.gov.uk/corporate/publications-and-reports/taxi-and-private-hire.

- The London Hackney Carriages Acts 1831, 1843 and 1853 regulate driver conduct, the grant of driver licences, and magistrates' court powers of revocation or suspension of the licence if the vehicle is not fit for purpose.

- The Metropolitan Public Carriage Act 1869 governs the grant of hackney carriage licences and the requirement that only a licensed driver can drive hackney carriages.

- The London Cab Order 1934 regulates applications, the grant and refusal of licences, and covers meters and fares.

- The London Cab Order 1972 allows a maximum journey of 20 miles for hackney carriages hired from Heathrow Airport.

25.13 Hackney carriage drivers' licences can be granted by a local authority for up to three years, although most are only granted for one year at a time to enable full oversight of the drivers and their medical and personal fitness for the job. To drive without a current hackney carriage licence (for example, where it has been suspended) is an offence, and the proprietor would also be liable if this were permitted.

25.14 To successfully apply for a hackney carriage licence, the applicant must, first, have held a drivers' licence for over 12 months before the date (not the grant) of the application and, second, be a 'fit and proper person'.

25.15 The test of 'fit and proper person' is a thorny issue. Local authorities will want to check for previous convictions, but they can also request other information and impose conditions that are reasonably considered to be necessary. This could include an additional driving test, a test of the local area, or a test of the applicant's standard of English. The applicant's general demeanour and behaviour can be taken into account; the honesty, sobriety and general trustworthiness of a hackney carriage driver are of paramount importance because of the impact upon passenger safety.

25.16 The Rehabilitation of Offenders Act 1974 (Exceptions) Order 1975 means that previous convictions are never 'spent' in the course of time, all remaining 'live' and needing to be fully disclosed and considered. Each local authority should have a policy about their approach to previous convictions. Case law confirms that the authority cannot go behind the fact of a conviction. Failure to comply with disclosure requirements is, of itself, a sign of unfitness, and the overriding consideration is always the protection of the public, which, of course, encourages authorities to be cautious when considering who can be trusted to provide public transport. One of the mainstays of the taxi industry is school and college transport, often for disabled children (or adults) who cannot access buses, and the test has to properly reflect the need to protect the most vulnerable members of society. Perhaps surprisingly, a conviction for sexual assault and inclusion on the Sex Offenders' Register is not an *automatic* bar to drive a taxi, although it seems unlikely that most authorities would consider such a person to be 'fit and proper'.

25.17 Ultimately, if appealed by the applicant, the final determination will be made by the magistrates' court[2]. Each case must be considered on its merits, and references from current employers, together with the loss of income and livelihood, should be taken into account.

PRIVATE HIRE VEHICLES

25.18 Private hire vehicles are a newer concept than hackney carriages, and only came into being in 1976. The crucial difference is that a private hire vehicle must be pre-booked. Such vehicles cannot ply for hire or wait for customers on a cab rank. Whilst hackney carriages are often required to be a certain type of vehicle – like the uniform London cabs – private hire vehicles can be just that, private vehicles used for hire, although they are heavily regulated nonetheless. In fact, they are not permitted to look like hackney carriages, as it must be easy to tell at a glance which is which.

25.19 The initial legislation was the Local Government (Miscellaneous Provisions) Act 1976 for private hire vehicles outside Greater London, which applies everywhere except in Plymouth where they have their own regulations. Greater London is governed by the Private Hire Vehicles (London) Act 1998, which is part of Transport for London, but the requirements are broadly the same.

25.20 Private hire vehicles, defined as a vehicle which can carry fewer than nine people, must be driven by someone who has a private hire drivers' licence from their local authority, and, crucially, there must be a private hire operator in the background who will take bookings, arrange collection, and set fares. The contract is between the person booking the ride and the operator, not the driver. The operator is responsible for making sure that the correct licences are in place for both the vehicles and drivers. No such operator is needed for hackney carriages who are, by definition, totally independent.

25.21 To complicate matters further, it has been held that no actual payment need be made for an agreement to amount to 'hiring in the course of business' for a private hire vehicle. It follows that, even if a car is not a licensed hire vehicle, it can still fall within this definition. This was established when a Mr Taylor, a

2   *Secretary of State for Transport, Local Government and the Regions v Snowdon* [2003] RTR 15.

private hire driver, asked his wife (who was not a licensed private hire driver) to fulfil a contractual obligation of his to take a booked passenger in her own car and without payment. The court held that this still amounted to 'hiring in the course of a business'[3].

25.22   There are exemptions, most notably under section 75(1)(b) of the Local Government (Miscellaneous Provisions) Act 1976 ('LG(MP)A 1976'), which provides a defence but only where there is:

(i)   a specific vehicle contracted out;

(ii)   for a defined period of more than seven days; and

(iii)   with a specified notice period for the contract to end.

25.23   Without these three conditions, an offence will have been committed, so great care must be taken, and there are further complications to be considered if the vehicle is used outside the contracted times for other hiring. Vehicles provided for transport for funerals or weddings are also exempt.

25.24   In summary, there are three licences needed, all of which must be issued by the same local authority:

(1)   Private Hire Operator's licence – the 'fit and proper person' test applies. The test is the same as that for hackney carriage drivers' licences, and the local authority (district council) are able to request any information which they reasonably deem to be necessary. The scope of this request is wide-ranging, but it is not possible to obtain an enhanced criminal record check for private hire operators (as opposed to drivers) because, as the organisers behind the business, they are not likely to have any contact with vulnerable people. Providing false or misleading information is an offence. Licences can last for up to five years, although they are often annual. Conditions can be imposed – for example, ensuring that there is sufficient parking at the operator's base address. Mandatory conditions include keeping detailed records of the journeys booked: where, when, and which driver, must all be noted and provided to the police upon request. Operators' licences can be suspended or revoked, or renewal can be refused (LG(MP)A 1976, s 62).

(2)   Private Hire Vehicle licence – the licence requires the vehicle to be in good roadworthy condition, and 'suitable' for such use. Details of ownership and usage must be included (as per LG(MP)A 1976, s 48). The vehicle must also carry a private hire plate. Again, conditions can be imposed and, once licensed, the vehicle can carry passengers anywhere in England and Wales. Vehicle licences can be suspended or revoked, or renewal can be refused.

3   *St Albans District Council v Taylor* [1991] Crim LR 852.

(3) Private Hire Driver's licence – the 'fit and proper person' test applies, and the driver must have had a full driving licence for at least a year. Just like hackney carriage drivers, a full CRB check is carried out, as well as checks with the DVLA. Beyond this, the local authority can impose any conditions which they think fit. The licence can be granted for up to three years, although in practice they are usually annual to enable more control by the authority. Just as with hackney carriages, the driver's licence can be suspended or revoked, or renewal can be refused (LG(MP)A 1976, s 61).

25.25 The systems for hackney carriages and private hire vehicles are both regulated and licensed by the local authority, who will take action against any breaches of conditions imposed on any of the applicable licences.

25.26 There are statutory rights of appeal to the magistrates' court against refusal to grant or renew, or a decision to revoke or suspend:

- a hackney carriage driver's licence;

- a private hire operator's licence;

- a private hire vehicle licence; or

- a private hire driver's licence.

25.27 Appeal against a failure to renew, or to suspend or revoke a hackney carriage proprietor's licence, also lies with the magistrates' court. Conversely, appeal against the refusal to *grant* a hackney carriage proprietor's licence is to the Crown Court.

Index

[All references are to paragraph numbers.]